TREASON AT WEST POINT:
The Arnold-André Conspiracy

Portrait of Benedict Arnold by Du Simetiere.
Courtesy of The Historical Society of Pennsylvania.

TREASON AT WEST POINT:
The Arnold-André Conspiracy

by

J.E. Morpurgo

MASON / CHARTER

NEW YORK 1975

Published simultaneously in the United Kingdom by Mason/Charter, London, England

First Printing

Printed in the United States of America

Library of Congress Cataloging in Publication Data

Morpurgo, J. E.
    Treason at West Point: the Arnold-André Conspiracy.

    (Great events in world history)
    Includes index.
    1. Arnold, Benedict, 1741-1801. 2. André, John, 1751-1780. I. Title.
E236.M67   973.3'82   75-1378
ISBN 0-88405-303-2

For my daughter

Katharine

Contents

List of Illustrations

1. Treason Doth Never Prosper

ON A SEPTEMBER night in 1780 two men met in a house close to the Hudson River. One, Major John André, was there to do no more than his duty as adjutant general of the British army under General Sir Henry Clinton. The other, Major General Benedict Arnold of the Continental Army, was present to complete arrangements for a sordid act of treachery, the handing-over of his command at West Point to the British and with it, as possible consequence, the severance of communications between New England and the Middle Atlantic States, thus insuring, almost certainly, the entire defeat of the American cause. A rendezvous between the two officers had been planned for some months in a series of letters signed by code names and exchanged by anonymous intermediaries. But the place where they actually met and the time of their meeting were forced on them by a sequence of accidents. These, with subsequent and trivial mishaps, were to bring about the ultimate tragic paradox: rank and wealth for the traitor and ignominious death at the end of a hangman's rope for the man of honor.

The shadow of disaster was already on them as they

1

talked that night. Yet, had they met in different circumstances, what they had in common might have bridged the gap between them. True, they came from opposing armies, but they had fought in the same campaigns and over the same territory; and it is not uncommon for soldiers to find the company of old enemies more congenial than the society of men who have never known war. Their origins were as different as their physical appearance. Arnold, the thick-set, swarthy American, was a New Englander with generation upon generation of Anglo-Saxon ancestors behind him; André, the tall, elegant British major had not one drop of English blood. But they had many mutual acquaintances. It was even rumored that they had loved the same girl, and certainly Arnold's wife was on friendly terms with André (which might not have made the two men comfortable in each other's company). Both Arnold and André had some experience of commerce but both preferred the glamor, the excitement, and the variety of soldiering to the drudgery of the countinghouse; and for all their love of uniforms, parties, and parades, both had proved themselves skilled and serious in the military arts and sciences. Both were sensitive—Arnold with the sensitivity of a man who for all his courage and bombast longed for others to share the high opinion that he had of himself and André with the sensitivity of an artist. Above all other similarities: both were ambitious.

Looking back through the centuries at the two men as they talked together, and with our knowledge of what was to come, it is not possible to feel anything but admiration and pity for John André and despising for Benedict Arnold. For all that, and from the very beginning of any consideration of the causes and consequences of that September meeting, it is vital that there be some attempt to revalue the implications of the conspiracy without too much heed to the weight of prejudice in both contemporary and subsequent opinion. Nothing can shift sympathy for André. Pity for him is heightened by the knowledge that his brilliance was snuffed out in an act of dubious justice, which brought no honor to George Washington or the Continental Army. Had André survived, his considerable promise would surely have brought him to high rank in the next decades when Britain stood, often alone, against the French Revolution and Bonaparte—a tyranny far more vicious than anything exercised by George III.

But, just because André was a good officer he knew something of the risks that were involved when he arranged to meet Arnold. "He was a man of honor" so runs the American folksong on the death of André. For an eighteenth-century officer, honor was as important as life itself, and had he known that this was to be the epitaph written for him by his country's enemies, André would have died, not content but comforted.

The case of Arnold is quite otherwise. He survived for 21 years after the discovery of his treachery, and among his contemporaries, both British and American, not the least of his offenses was that he lived and André died. (Again the ballad: "And everyone wished him released and Arnold in his stead.") He was reviled by those whom he had betrayed and often despised by those whom he had sought to serve. He died a lonely and disappointed man. To this day, his is the dishonor of standing first in the list of American traitors, and from 1780 on his name became for Americans a synonym for treachery.

The betrayal of country and comrades-in-arms has always been considered among the most vile of crimes and no rationalization can restore Arnold's reputation. Even so, there are reasons for some hesitation before the condemnation by his contemporaries and American mythology can be accepted as unshakable and final.

First, his actions must be considered against the background of the American Revolution, and secondly, with that background still in mind, some thought must be given to the nature of treason as it has been interpreted through the centuries in many countries.

American popular opinion has persisted in looking back to the Revolution as a struggle between a righteous, unshakably noble cause and the arrogant forces of oppression. This was not the way it was seen by all contemporaries, not even by all Americans, while the war was being fought. For many, at the time, it was a civil war during which men of conscience on both sides of the Atlantic argued, plotted, and went to battle for what they believed to be right. In Britain as in America opinion was divided, and there was in the 13 colonies-turned-states a substantial minority of Americans who hoped for reconciliation with Great Britain. None other than the second president of the United States, John Adams, gave it as his opinion that one million of the three million colonials were Loyalists, and throughout his life Adams never accepted as undeniable doctrine the idea that monarchy and Americanism were essentially incompatible. Five years before the meeting between Arnold and André, before the first shots were fired in the American Revolution, John Adams had written:

> We are part of the British Dominions, that is of the King of Great Britain. And it is our interest and duty to continue subject to the authority of Parliament in the regulation of our trade, as long as she shall leave us to govern our internal policy. . . .

And, a month later, another of the great leaders of America, Benjamin Franklin, wrote:

> I would try anything, and bear anything that can be borne with safety to our just principles rather than engage in a war with such relations unless compelled to in dire necessity in our own defence.

Even the *Declaration of Causes of Taking Up Arms,* drafted in part by Thomas Jefferson and issued on July 6, 1775, held to the belief that war did not mean the end of the British connection:

> We have not raised armies with ambitious designs of separating from Great Britain and establishing independent States . . . we must devoutly implore His Divine Goodness to protect us happily through this great conflict, to dispose our adversaries to reconciliation on reasonable terms, and thereby to relieve the empire from the calamities of civil war.

The battle years between 1775 and 1780 had hardened attitudes; but in areas of New Jersey, Delaware, Maryland, and on the frontiers of Georgia and the Carolinas some people remained ardently Loyalist. One American author described Pennsylvania as "enemy's country"; and in New York many of the great families and not a few humbler people were for the king. Again it was John Adams who said of Pennsylvania and New York "that if New England on one side and Virginia on the other had not kept them in awe, they would have joined the British." There were everywhere Loyalists, many secret, and some (even in the most ardently Revolutionary communities) like John Randolph in Virginia, who never deigned to hide their continued devotion to king and Parliament. Whenever there was a British victory, some secret Loyalists made public their partiality, and in 1780 when the American cause was at a low ebb, a considerable number even among the patriots were tired of war or convinced that by war they had already achieved enough to force on the British a compromise solution. For the British, too, were divided, and no less than the Americans, troubled by factions at home and by a powerful and vocal minority which supported the American cause and looked to see American grievances removed.

By that time, new grievances had sprung up in America, not caused by the British but by growing distaste for politicians and profiteers, and by inevitable doubts in the minds of thinking Americans about the ultimate justice of winning a war against British despotism only because they had massive aid from a despotism far worse than anything Britain had ever exercised: the despotism of the French Crown.

For all these grievances and doubts, for this exhaustion and for this division of loyalty, Benedict Arnold could have provided a cure. Hand over West Point, end the war, and seek a sensible peace that would give the American colonies a measure of independence under the Crown, something after the fashion proposed already in 1766 by Richard Bland of Virginia, something after the fashion of the dominion status that Canada, Australia, South Africa, and New Zealand were to achieve.

Though the name of Benedict Arnold cannot be placed firmly either with those who in conscience opposed the Revolution or with those who were eager for compromise, though his motives were almost certainly self-centered, it was the existence of these substantial groups which gave some kind of justification for his change of heart and coat, and which, had his venture been successful, would have blotted out any suggestion that he had behaved improperly. Had Arnold's actions brought an end to the Revolution he would have been acclaimed a hero by many Americans who believed that their duty to their sovereign was greater than any grievance against Britain and far outstripped any sense of responsibility to their neighbors. He would have been forgiven by many more Americans who, unwilling though they may have been to take up arms against the American cause, were nevertheless not entirely convinced of the moral and legal correctness of rebellion or of the political and economic wisdom of breaking with Britain. Even among those ardent and active on the American side, Arnold's success would have found many who believed that complete victory was beyond achievement, who would have welcomed an excuse to make peace on good terms. Among the British, the majority would have seen Arnold as the means whereby the proper conscience of America had been revived, and even many in the considerable minority in Britain which supported the American Revolution would have felt that the Americans had made their point as true Britons and could now be restored to the British family.

Treason doth never prosper. What's the reason?
For if it prosper none dare call it treason.
(Sir John Harrington, Epigrams)

Thus, a sixteenth-century couplet by a wit who had seen many great and good men changing sides; but even that epigram implies fear as a hold against accusations of treachery. And to map the boundary line between reason and conscience, between loyalty and betrayal, is a task that cannot be measured with the simple arithmetic of fear.

The Constitution has it directly and simply:

> Treason against the United States shall consist only in levying war against them, or in adhering to their Enemies, giving them Aid and Comfort.

Directly and simply, or so it seems until one realizes first, that as significant comment upon the Arnold case the Constitution is irrelevant for it was not yet written, and the United States did not yet exist. Even had it been written, the definition of treason in the Constitution is little different from that contained in the manifestoes of every rebel group and the constitution not only of every democracy but also of every despotic regime in history.

Historical analogies are never complete, for no two events are similar, but if there is to be understanding of the ambiguous nature of treason and, more immediately, some readjustment, however minute, to the universal condemnation of Arnold, then it is useful to set down without too much comment a short series of statements and questions about some conspiracies that have been judged treasonable or might have been so judged had they failed.

For example, was it treasonable when Brutus and his fellow Romans decided to cut down Caesar?

> Fashion it thus; that what he is, augmented,
> Would run to these and these extremities.
> (Shakespeare. *Julius Caesar,* Act II, Scene 1)

Were those German officers who attempted to murder Hitler traitors to their nation or were they subscribing to a loyalty greater than devotion to the State?

Were Robert E. Lee and Jefferson Davis traitors?

Much of the distaste for Arnold is founded upon his breaking the Oath of Allegiance taken at Valley Forge in 1778. A similar accusation could be, and indeed was, levelled at Robert E. Lee, but though Lee's cause, like Arnold's, was defeated, his reputation as one of the truly honorable men of American history remains undimmed. It is possible to argue in defense of Arnold that an oath to undertake rebellion is no oath at all, and had he achieved his ends he could have turned upon many, even of the most revered, of American leaders, George Washington among them, who by the very act of rebellion had either implicitly or explicitly broken their oaths of allegiance to the Crown.

The regime at present in power in Rhodesia has used in its own support much of the vocabulary of the American Revolution, yet almost universally it is condemned as a rebel government. And the question stands as to whether a Rhodesian indulging in an attempt to reinstate the rightful authority would be hero or traitor?

The closest historical analogy to Arnold's case is that of General George Monck who, in 1660, changed sides, brought back Charles II from exile, and thus ended the long-standing Cromwellian "rebellion." The difference between the two stories is that Monck was successful.

Had Arnold's conspiracy succeeded, his name would have gone into the history books as one of the truly inspired men of the English-speaking peoples. But Arnold's plot failed, and the fame that he had coveted turned to infamy that perversely has kept his name familiar to Americans long after they have forgotten all but a very few of his equals among the generals of the American Revolution.

Yet for his contemporaries, both American and British, the sum of Arnold's actions in 1780 was not only a matter of treachery, nor yet of failure to accomplish the ends that he had sought. For Americans and British alike, one consequence of his attempted treason and of his failure made him incomparably villainous: the death of his fellow conspirator, John André.

2. John André

PERHAPS ONCE in every generation a minor character thrusts all major actors from the center stage of events. For a moment his charm, his strength, his comedy, or his tragedy, becomes the focal point of attention and, through the concentration of topical interest, holds for that moment the attention of historians. All turn toward him and even his most eminent contemporaries step aside to look at him. Then, as he moves from the stage, the ephemeral success of the small-part player vanishes before the arrogance of true and imagined grandeur.

It was thus with John André. While he stood trial for his life his small scene held the progress of the far greater drama and the great personalities of the American Revolution—Washington, Lafayette, Alexander Hamilton, Benedict Arnold, Sir Henry Clinton, and Lord George Germain—became mere supports to André's part, their status twisted to the curved mirror of his suffering. Then with his death the stilled logic of history was jerked back to life; more urgent issues than the fate of one comparatively junior British officer regained their full significance and, in the tragi-comedy of the end of one empire and the epic of the beginning of another, André's fine, bitter moment of melodrama was obscured and almost forgotten.

A plaque on a house in Bath where he once stayed,

a lonely memorial in Tappan, New York, an American folk ballad in his honor, a casual mention in an essay by Charles Lamb, a place in the regimental histories of three British infantry regiments, and a series of footnotes by authorities on military law are almost all that remain to his memory. These things and a hideous monument among the cluster of hideous monuments in Westminster Abbey—almost unnoticed by Englishmen but noticed by visiting Americans who marvel that a man hanged as a spy should have found a place among the poets, the statesmen, the generals, and the admirals whose memorials fill Britain's hall of honor. Yet, even had he not made his one tragic appearance in the great moment of crisis for the American Revolution, still John André would be a fascinating representative of a type that belongs especially to the eighteenth century: the dilettante, the man of remarkably varied enthusiasms and magnificently versatile accomplishments. Handsome, courageous, witty, in his short adult life, he seemed to have the capacity for living 25 hours in every 24. He was a sound regular soldier, more spirited than many, considerably more intelligent than most, and his short career stands as evidence that if the eighteenth-century British War Office was disastrously inclined to find well-polished pegs for nonexistent holes, British generals in the field were not all so slow to recognize ability as the history books have made out. He was a good linguist and a skillful military draftsman—both important additions to his qualifications as an officer, but beyond this he was a poet, an artist, an actor, and—not least significant as prelude to the events at West Point—a gallant, a ladies man who could charm even an American bird into the British woods.

John André was born in London on May 2, 1750. (It

is interesting that he and, after his death, his family tried to make his romantic youthfulness even more romantic by subtracting a year from his age, so that even the memorial in Westminster Abbey has him as 29 years old at the moment of his death.) His father, Anthony, came originally from Geneva where he had been at the university. Soon after he finished his education, Anthony André settled in England and took up business "in the Levantine trade" from Warnford Court, Throgmorton Street, close by where the Bank of England now stands in the center of the old City of London. He married Marie Girardot, like himself a French Protestant, whose family, though still maintaining a house in Paris, had long associations with England. On March 25, 1748, Anthony André became a naturalized British subject.

John was Anthony's first son. The family, in which there were eventually five children—two boys and three girls—lived a life of middle-class prosperity and increasingly English style. But, as John grew up, from his father and mother and from their many Huguenot friends in England (there were at the time more than 20 French Huguenot churches in London) he learned not only French but also Italian and German.

One trait in the character of the adult John André, his fierce loyalty to Britain and in particular to the monarchy, can be readily traced to this family background of Continental Protestantism. Here, perhaps, is another response to the question "What is treason?"; the question "What makes loyalty?" Popular myth, especially in America, has never conceded the degree to which Britain was a melting pot long before the United States existed (and still in the centuries after). Though many of the leaders of the American Revolution did recognize that Britain was a refuge of liberty much sought after by the persecuted minorities of Europe (and indeed held as one of their major grievances that freedoms readily accorded to immigrants from the Continent were denied to American colonials), their successors seldom appreciate that for the Protestant minorities in Catholic countries in the seventeenth and eighteenth centuries Britain was the promised land. For those who escaped persecution for their faith, and above all for the Huguenots, who for almost two centuries had fitted easily into the English way of life, gratitude to the nation which had given them both refuge and comfort was natural and more likely to breed fierce devotion than home-grown patriotism.

Only five years before John André was born the House of Stuart had made an attempt to overthrow the ruling House of Hanover. To a Huguenot family, the Catholic Young Pretender's invasion, launched with the assistance of the Catholic king of France, must have been a nightmare and the victory of George II a cause for great rejoicing. The Young Pretender, though after 1745 a broken man, did in fact outlive John André by eight years, and there were throughout his life from time to time minor murmurings of support for his cause.

In France itself, when John André was born, the Huguenots were still an oppressed minority. He was already 12 years old when Jean Calas, a Huguenot merchant of Toulouse, was put to death by being broken on the wheel, merely because the Catholic rabble demanded his execution on the grounds that he must have been responsible for the suicide of his son, a Catholic. Such an event would have been discussed by the Andrés, who still had relatives in Paris, and its horrors would have given them even more cause for contrasting their own ease and liberty with the miseries of their co-religionists abroad. Later in his life, when André was in North America, he never questioned the righteousness of the British cause, not even when he was serving under Sir William Howe, a British general who showed some sympathy for American grievances. For André the Americans were in rebellion against a benevolent monarchy, and they were supported, even controlled, by the Catholic French.

Though for family and business reasons the André parents held to some of their Continental connections, they gave to their children a thoroughly English education. John went first to a day school near his home, much patronized by the aristocracy, Mr Newcome's school at Hackney, and then to St Paul's School, the great school "in the shadow of the Cathedral" which had educated John Milton, Samuel Pepys, and the Duke of Marlborough. Sadly, no record remains of his school days; only his own statement and a persisting tradition settles the place of his education, for his name does not appear in the (admittedly incomplete) St Paul's School registers. Even so, if as seems likely, André left St Paul's in 1767, it is surprising that when only 13 years later he became a national hero, the memorial notices which appeared in all the journals were devastatingly vague about his youth.

Indeed, very little about John André is certain until he worked at his father's business at "a desk by a small coal-fire in a gloomy compting house in Warnford Court."

Even his father's death in April 1769 did not release John from this business for which he was never suited and which he never liked; but the practice of trade had not then that 9 a.m. to 6 p.m., five-days-a-week monotony with which it has since become plagued. Only a few weeks after his father's death, John with his mother, sisters, and young brother, left London for a long holiday at Matlock in Derbyshire. There, though John André did not actually come into contact with the great, for the first time he became friendly with some who had great men among their acquaintances.

Matlock was a spa, beautifully set in hilly country. It was in the eighteenth century essentially a middle-class resort and here the prosperous bourgeoisie sought health and amusement. And at Matlock, between baths, taking of the waters, and sedate parties, the Andrés became friendly with the Seward family.

The Sewards came from Lichfield, the small cathedral city in Staffordshire, and by one of those strange accidents for which history can offer no satisfactory explanation, Lichfield was at that time the center and the source of intellectual energy and eminence far beyond its potential as expressed in terms of size, previous, or subsequent glory.

Canon Seward lived in the Bishop's Palace (the Bishop's luxurious tastes rather than his pastoral responsibilities persuading him to prefer other places of residence). Canon Seward was a minor poet of little power and great conceit. His wife was the daughter of the Reverend John Hunter, that master of the Lichfield Grammar School who had taught Lichfield's two greatest living sons: Dr Samuel Johnson and the actor-playwright, David Garrick. Hunter, according to Johnson, was "a man very skilful in a little way," he flogged efficiently and unmercifully "to save you from the gallows."

The Sewards' elder daughter, Anna, was already 27 years old at the time of the Matlock holiday and already a versifier whose work was so much better than her father's that in comparison it seemed to be poetry. Her work was eventually to be edited by Sir Walter Scott who also wrote the epitaph for her tomb in Lichfield Cathedral and only saved his reputation as a judge of literature by his treacherous and private comment to a friend that most of her poetry "is absolutely execrable."

Close to the Seward family was the greatest of Lichfield's residents, Dr. Erasmus Darwin, physician, philosopher, poet, founder of the Lunar Society, reformer, humanitarian, teetotaler, evolutionist (long before his greater grandson, Charles), and dreamer of a thousand mad ideas that have become in the course of time everyday sanity.

Among those who came to Lichfield to see Darwin were the engineer Matthew Boulton, the great philanthropist and potter Josiah Wedgwood, and William Small, formerly professor of natural philosophy and mathematics at the College of William and Mary in Virginia, a man who, according to Thomas Jefferson, "fixed the destinies of my life."

And, as a result of the Matlock holiday, John André came to Lichfield to stay with the Sewards.

In later years, when André's reputation in the British army and among his American enemies depended as much on his excellence as a dilettante as on his efficiency as a soldier, that reputation was founded upon the casual but advanced education he had gleaned by eavesdropping in Lichfield more than upon the formal and narrow training of Newcome's, St. Paul's and perhaps, the University of Geneva.

Many of the visitors to the Bishop's Palace were members also of Darwin's Lunar Society. These men were observers of life a little, and of nature much, and

they knew how to describe and harness their observa-
tions. The actual attainments of Darwin, for example,
great as they seemed to his contemporaries, now seem
infinitesimal and prosaic when compared to the attainments of some of his fellow visitors such as Joseph
Priestley, James Watt, or even Matthew Boulton. But
the spur of curiosity was at them all, and it was this same
urgent curiosity, the finest of all weapons for a soldier
whose peculiar genius was to be shown on special
missions, which gave John André the inspiration for his
bustling career as an army officer. They were wits too (in
this none outshone Darwin himself) and in their
company, and in silence, André learned the art of quick
conversational exchange which the eighteenth century
treasured beyond all other arts and which he was to use
to such effect even in the awesome last days of his life.

André was invited to Lichfield at the suggestion of
the third Seward girl, one who was a member of the
family in everything but name, Honora Sneyd. But his
intellectual curiosity drove him much into the company
of Anna, so much so that a particularly attentive Robert
Lovell Edgeworth later remarked "From the great
attention that Miss Seward paid to him and from the
constant admiration which Mr. André bestowed on her it
seemed there might exist some courtship between
them."

Anna was John André's senior by eight years, a
disproportion that has never prevented a 19-year-old
from falling in love, but she was fat, almost obese, a
condition which usually does deter youth. Honora had
no brains, but great beauty; John André had good looks
and undoubtedly thought that he could supply enough
in the way of intelligence to satisfy both their needs. It

was Honora with whom he was soon dramatically in love.

Honora Sneyd had been five when, orphaned, she had come to live with the Sewards. Anna adored her, all the family and most of their friends cossetted her, and once she reached adolescence she was surrounded by young men, and men not so young, who imagined themselves in love with her. John André was just one in the middle of a long queue.

Honora for her part was attracted to him. Women, of all ages, found it difficult to avoid being attracted to John André. But it is doubtful if Honora, from whom even the kindliness of time cannot remove a suspicion of silliness, was then or ever after capable of love. Certainly she could not fall in love with a young man, however good looking, who had no prospects. André's heart went out to Honora in letters of unhesitating ardor and great length, but the love screeds went by way of Anna, and it was in the covering letters to Anna that he unburdened his dissatisfaction with his enforced profession of merchant.

History does not resist a good coincidence. When John André was writing to Anna Seward of his great ambition to do something that would make his name for all time and complaining of his misery as he sat over "the desk's dead wood," 3,000 miles away another clerk, even younger than André, was writing in much the same sense and using some almost identical expressions.

I contemn the grovelling condition of a desk to which my fortune condemns me and would willingly risk my life, though not my character, to exalt my station; I mean to prepare the way for futurity.

Those lines were written by Alexander Hamilton, and Hamilton, his station by then much exalted, was with André in his last tragic hours.

Throughout the second half of 1769 and on into 1770 John André maintained his correspondence with Lichfield: love letters to Honora, confused ponderings about the future to Anna. The great Miss Seward was herself confused. For all her intelligence and for all the fame of her poetry she was essentially a provincial, maiden aunt with a zest for matchmaking. She looked fondly on the two handsome young people, her much loved, adopted sister, and the brilliant young man from London; and she dreamed of their marriage almost as if it were to be her own. But although she seldom mentioned it, she knew that Honora was pampered and would not have a husband who could not afford the money and the time to continue spoiling her. And John was forever telling her that for his sanity he must leave the business his father had bequeathed to the family and forever asking her what profession he should adopt. The only professions with which Anna was at all familiar were the Church and poetry. As the Church of England was closed to André by his Huguenot faith, Anna encouraged him toward poetry for which he did show some aptitude. Anna gave him poetic exercises, but even she knew that few poets can buy elegant gowns for their wives exclusively out of the proceeds of poetry, and so Anna and John began to exchange other ideas. A Member of Parliament? Perhaps; but that too needed money. An artist! André was very clever with a pencil, but artists, like poets, are notoriously poor. A soldier? Several times they came back to this possibility. But always between André and the advice he received from Anna and other distinguished Lichfielders, whose conversation had helped to arouse his dissatisfaction with a future as a middle-aged merchant "in a bob-wig, a rough beard, in snuff-coloured clothes, grasping a guinea in his hand," stood Honora. Though she had not decided to accept him as her husband she was not going to encourage him too much in his foolishness in case nothing better turned up, and she certainly was not going to agree to marry any young man whose income was precariously obtained by poetry, soldiering, or even politics. "I know she has a fervent wish to see me a quill-driver," John wrote to Anna and then in the same letter still addressed to Anna, "But, oh my dear Honora—it is for Thy sake only I wish for wealth." Almost he persuaded himself that Honora was right, though still he wrote (to Anna):

I have now completely subdued my aversion to the profession of merchant, and hope in time to acquire an inclination for it. . . . When an impertinent consciousness whispers in my ear that I am not of the right stuff for a merchant, I draw my Honora's picture from my bosom, and the sight of that dear talisman so inspirits my industry that no toil appears oppressive.

But it could not last. John André was not made of the right stuff for the business of bills of lading, of accounts, of debits and credits. His mind was seldom at his desk. He scribbled clever caricatures in the margins of his letters; he turned from his ledgers to improve the verses that he had written in his notebook; he thought of Honora; and with an intensity that seems almost prophetic he considered the grim prospect that, unless he moved soon, his name might never appear in the histories.

Other and richer rivals were courting Honora.

André, beginning to realize the hopelessness of his case, turned to some of his London friends and particularly to a contemporary, another Huguenot, Peter Boissier, who was enjoying himself hugely as an officer in the 11th Dragoons. Legend has insisted that André joined the army because Honora Sneyd jilted him. She did not jilt him; she just never made up her mind to accept him.

And so on March 4, 1771, John André was commissioned as a second lieutenant in the Seventh of Foot, later the Royal Fusiliers.

As was the custom of the time André bought his commission. There was as yet in Britain (as in most countries) no school for preparing officers. Once appointed, their regimental duties in peace time consisted of little more than ceremonial gyrations ceremoniously carried out under the guidance of noncommissioned officers and social exercises conducted according to the custom of their regiment and the manners of their class. Junior officers in the British army in the eighteenth century were expected to be soldiers by instinct and, as they were gentlemen by origin and upbringing, it was assumed that in action they would know how to lead and, if all else failed, would know how to die. Experience was the only military training ground that the eighteenth century understood and it was assumed, with some justice, that any officer who survived one battle would learn from it some lesson which would be of use to him in the next, until by surviving enough battles—and having enough money or a sufficiency of influential friends to win promotion—eventually he would rise to command. To observers from later centuries this method seems wasteful, inefficient, and undemocratic. Yet, to a point it worked. The British army in the eighteenth century had its share

Major John André in uniform. Reprinted from *Political Magazine,* 1781.

of stupid, arrogant, and lazy officers, but somehow it also thrust forward into positions of command rather more than its share of incomparable leaders, among them Marlborough, Wolfe, Sir John Moore, and Wellington.

As for John André, who had little money and no friends in high places, almost from the beginning of his military career the army treated him as an officer out of the ordinary. In very short time he had trained himself in the elementary military arts; from the general evidence of the period it is almost certain that he found no one else to do it for him. But, just as there was then no military school in which a young officer could acquire the rudiments of his profession, so also was there no staff college, nor any systematic method whereby the army could select and prepare officers for those appointments in administration, the control of operations, and intelligence work—all of which were scarcely less important in the eighteenth century than they are today. Yet, by what process we do not know, André was selected for the staff and set to learning, again by the one means the eighteenth century knew: experience. After only a few months as a regimental officer, drinking hard at the traditions of the service, the regiment (and such other drinks as he could afford), André was sent off on a special mission to Germany. Except for two short spells, and although for administrative purposes his name was twice transferred to the lists of other regiments, he never again served as an ordinary infantry officer.

It is tempting to assume the cloak of the thrill writer and to argue back through André's subsequent short but professionally sensational career to the point where it can be suggested that even as early as 1772 the authorities had André cast for the part of staff officer in the army's intelligence service. For once, falling to

temptation seems justifiable. That first mission to
Germany was almost certainly a humdrum exercise, the
kind of work that is now the everyday business of military
attachés: the by-no-means-secret assessment of the
strength, dispositions, training methods, strategic and
tactical philosophies of foreign armies. But it was a
beginning and, if nothing else, his selection proves that
the army had taken note of his linguistic skill, his ability
as a draftsman, his powers of expression, and perhaps
also his engaging personality which allowed him to make
friends not only among military men but also among
thinkers, talkers, and their womenfolk.

What followed upon his German adventure is also
shadowy, but in the shadows there is apparent still more
evidence that André was being treated by his superiors as
something outside the ordinary run of junior officers.
His regiment had been ordered to Canada and late in
1773 André was given instructions to join his fellow
officers in Quebec. Yet it was nine months before he set
out across the Atlantic.

First, he went home to England, where he spent
much time in the kind of society that he had never
before known, among politicians, senior officers and
"men of the world." He did go to Lichfield to see Anna
Seward. His ardor for Honora had not disappeared,
though temporarily it had faded before the excitement of
his new profession—happily for André because Richard
Lovell Edgeworth had proposed to make Honora his
second wife and she had accepted. In July 1773 the
marriage had been performed.

Yet this end to his one-time dream was not the
reason for André's long stay in England. If he felt sorrow
at all he made up for it with a round of parties in Bath
and in London. More than likely André was being

briefed for his next mission. When eventually he set sail in the summer of 1774 he did not take ship directly to Quebec as did his prospective commander, Sir Guy Carleton, nor even to Boston or New York. Instead, he sailed for Philadelphia and, once arrived, again showed none of the dutiful alacrity that might have been expected of a very junior subaltern on his way to rejoin his regiment. Instead, armed with the best introductions, he began a lengthy tour of Atlantic seaboard military headquarters and the cities of Pennsylvania, New Jersey, New York, and New England.

If, as seems likely, André was acting under orders, gathering impressions, information and acquaintances, nothing in his behavior or in the behavior of those who sent him can be regarded as in any way reprehensible. A British officer traveling through British North America was entirely within his rights, and the military establishment would have failed in its duty had it not taken every opportunity to investigate conditions, loyalties, and military possibilities in a land which was torn by disagreements between Americans and Americans and between Americans and the British. Already in 1770 in Boston, argument had deteriorated into riot. In the very month when John André landed in Philadelphia and in that very city, delegates from all the American colonies except Georgia were gathered together in an attempt to decide the manner of colonial opposition to overweening rule from London. Some thought to write petitions; some considered that they could win the day by boycotting British goods; a few, a very few, wanted to start a bloody rebellion. There was nothing secret about the debates; but many Americans still held close the secrets of their ultimate loyalty, and many more had not as yet tipped the scales of their own consciences. There was much for an intelligent observer to consider, much for him to discover by talking and listening, much for him to store in his mind for possible use in the immediate or the distant future.

Whatever it was that André saw and did during his extended tour of the colonies he reported ultimately to the governor of Massachusetts, General Thomas Gage, and then, at last, moved on into Canada to join his regiment.

There was in Canada little opportunity for those social relaxations which enlivened regimental duty at home, and which André had indulged with such charm in Germany and in the larger cities of the colonies. The whole force available to General Carleton was only 700 strong and, apart from a few in the garrisons of Montreal and Quebec, most of the men were stationed in primitive forts. Within weeks of his arrival in Canada André and his companions knew that they must prepare themselves to meet an attack. The long-smouldering fuse had burst into flames; the debate was over; the American colonies were under arms against Britain; their threats, their promises to the Canadians (who would have little to do with them), and the logic of military strategy insisted that the Americans must soon invade Lower Canada.

There were raids across an undefended frontier but the fullscale invasion was delayed, partly because two ambitious American officers—Ethan Allen and Benedict Arnold—were quarreling about who should command it. Then in the fall of 1775 Arnold began his great march through the wilderness toward Quebec, and American forces renewed active operations along the Sorel River with the object of capturing Montreal. At Fort Chambly, a small British force surrendered to the Americans commanded by General Richard Montgomery. Among the prisoners taken at Chambly was John André.

The surrender of Fort Chambly—and a few days later of other small forts on the Sorel River—confused the victors almost as much as it confounded their enemies. The thrust of events had hurled the American colonies into war without giving them pause to establish any effective organization for a nation or its army. Indeed, a substantial number even of those who were enthusiastic for war were far from enthusiastic about the idea of a central government or a unified army. Leaders and followers alike, their loyalties were to the colony from which they came, not to some nation that did not yet exist; and to them the idea, for example, of New Yorkers being subjected to the orders of a Virginian or of Pennsylvanians being disciplined by Marylanders seemed little if any improvement upon the subservience to the British which they were contesting. Amidst the excitements, frustrations, and arguments of the early months of the Revolution no one had thought to organize a system for the inconceivable: the reception of British prisoners of war.

However, if there were in the eighteenth century much brutality, there was also a code of military behavior that was part of the inheritance of both sides in the war. Whether out of a genuine sense of chivalry or from the sensible proposition that it is better to do for others what tomorrow they may have a chance to do for you, the effect was the same, and prisoners of war were generally treated to as much courtesy and as little discomfort as the circumstances of the capturing army would permit.

By André's own account the surrender at Chambly was not conducted with appropriate eighteenth-century decorum. He complained that he was stripped of his possessions except a miniature of his "beloved Honora" which he retained by hiding it in his mouth—an unlikely story and a hiding place unsuitable for one of André's vociferous disposition. But the irregular behavior was short lived. Apart from their liberty, all that the men of the Seventh of Foot lost was a regimental standard which was rushed off to Philadelphia where the politicians could gloat over it as a symbol of the triumphs of their men in the field and be persuaded to keep those men well supplied for future triumphs. For the rest, the officers were allowed to keep their side arms, it was agreed that officers and men would not be separated, and André was sent under parole back to the British base camp to collect baggage and funds for both officers and men so that their time of captivity should not be too uncomfortable or too much of an expense to their captors.

For more than a year André was a prisoner of war in central Pennsylvania. Though it must have been a frustrating period for a ambitious young officer, his experience had little in common with the experience of prisoners in more recent wars. For most of the time André was in the company of his closest regimental friend, Edward Despard. (It is yet another of the coincidences in the André story that Despard too was to be executed, though in much more shameful circumstances than André). The two officers lived either in taverns or in private houses. Although on at least two occasions their lives were threatened by local extremists they were for the most part treated with kindness and sometimes with warm hospitality by those who were either genuinely well disposed toward the British or who, in that uncertain time, saw the advantages of buttering bread on both sides. There were also, particularly among the Pennsylvania Quakers, some who because they discovered Despard and André to be courteous and palpably honest in their loyalties, treated the two officers as friends who by the accident of birth happened to have political views different from their own. Not a few, especially among the younger women, found the charm, elegance, and sophistication of the two young men a novelty and a delight when compared with the habitual earnestness of their neighbors. André, in particular, endeared himself to those, who were in effect his guards, by his wit and by his skill as an artist.

For most of his 14 months as a prisoner of war André was allowed considerable freedom of movement. He could sketch almost anything he saw, talk to whomever he met, and write letters whenever he wished providng they did not contain any comment on American affairs. No regulation could prevent him from noticing the many disagreements among the Americans about the conduct of the war or from holding in his retentive mind the names of those who spoke for the various factions. When, for example, orders reached Lancaster that the captive officers should be separated from their men, thus overturning the agreement made at Chambly, it was to Edward Shippen, the head of the local committee of safety, that André protested. Shippen upheld the protest and ignored the instructions from Philadelphia. The Shippen family was to figure centrally in the rest of the André story.

When finally in December 1776 André was to be exchanged he wrote to one of his American friends a letter which, even allowing for the conventional high-flowing courtesies of the eighteenth century, does demonstrate the closeness of the relationships which he had made with many in Pennsylvania:

> We are on our road (as we believe to be exchang'd) and however happy this prospect may make me, it doth not render me less warm in the fate of those persons in this Country for whom I had conceiv'd a regard. I trust on your side you will do me the justice to remember me with some good will . . . .

André rejoined the reconstituted Seventh of Foot, now stationed in New York under the command of General Sir William Howe.

Within weeks the subaltern submitted to the general a detailed report on conditions in Pennsylvania and with it included his personal recommendations for the future conduct of the war. Another few weeks, though there were no vacancies for a captain in the Seventh, and without purchasing his promotion, André was advanced in rank. For administrative purposes he was transferred to the Twenty-sixth of Foot (later the Cameronians) but his infantry days were over; Howe appointed him staff officer to one of his best divisional commanders, Major General Charles Grey.

As such André was responsible for the intelligence of the advance guard in Howe's strange campaign which led eventually to the fall of Philadelphia.

Then, and in the months when he was in Philadelphia, Howe's failure to destroy Washington's army when he seemed to have it at his mercy brought him much abuse from his contemporaries. The Scottish poet, Robert Burns, had his say:

> Poor Tommy Gage within a cage
> Was kept in Boston ha', man,
> Till Willie Howe took o'er the knowe,
> For Philadelphia, man
> Wi sword and gun he thought a sin
> Guid Christian blood to draw, man:
> But at New York, wi' knife and fork,
> Sir-loin he hacked sma', man.

Even his enemies criticized Howe's military ability. Lafayette describes his dilatoriness as the greatest fault of the British "during a war in which they committed so many errors." Yet Howe's earlier career had shown him skillful and decisive, and there is some reason for assuming that Howe's failure to destroy Washington's "ragged, lousy, naked regiments" was carefully calculated. With the American capital, Philadelphia, at his mercy, and in the knowledge that the two other major cities of the colonies, New York and Boston, were safely in British hands, Howe assumed that the Revolution was almost over. A ruthless campaign would add an unnecessary number to the casualty lists of both sides, would strengthen American determination to offer last-ditch resistance, and would make difficult the task of eventual reconciliation. What is more, he had good reason for believing that the harsh Pennsylvania winter would bring the Americans to their dutiful senses more effectively than could any vigorous military chastisement. (As the American army froze at Valley Forge and came very close to mutiny and as Congress sheltered ignominiously at York, where general complained against general and politician quarreled with politician, Howe must have thought his lack of action well justified.)

For a general in the field to take to himself political decisions that run counter to his orders is, in itself, a form of treason. Howe's dilatoriness, his failure to press home the advantages that the British had gained, was as close as he would come to deliberate disobedience, but it was close enough to serve as yet another example of the befuddlement of conscience that was aroused by the Revolution. The general was a Whig, sturdily opposed to the administration in London. He had spoken out roundly for the redress of American grievances. He had not wanted to command British armies against British subjects. His eldest brother, now dead but whose memory was still revered by Americans, had been a hero of the French and Indian War. He himself liked and was liked by most of the Americans he met. Therefore, he did his duty, by his own lights, and no more. At all events his letter of resignation was already on the way to Britain.

His subordinate, General Grey, was a man of a different stamp, by no means brutal but sternly professional and untouched by political considerations. Grey's intelligence officer, Captain André, was alert to the wider implications of military activity, but only as was appropriate to his task, insofar as they touched the immediate military objective. He knew that the loyalties of Pennsylvania in general, and of Philadelphians in particular, were divided. His duty, as the British advanced on Philadelphia, was to build up a day-to-day picture of American dispositions for his general with the aid of sympathetic informants. This he did with exemplary efficiency, and his situation reports enabled his commanding officer to organize some of the few brilliant operations in a campaign in which neither side demonstrated much ingenuity—including a night attack which has earned a vicious reputation in American history as the "Paoli Massacre" of General Anthony Wayne's forces, but which was in truth an operation of a kind that in later wars was to bring much glory to British Commandos and American Rangers.

On September 25, 1777, the British entered Philadelphia, and for a while it seemed that the city's history, both distant and recent, had been swept away. This was the Quaker City. Only 50 years earlier a mayor of Philadelphia had expressed horror because a group of wandering players had set up a stage just outside the city limits, and with the aid of the "sober people" had attempted to suppress the theater. Such bigotry had diminished since 1723, but still, until the arrival of the conquering British army, the sobriety of the Society of Friends was in Philadelphia a major influence; if no longer all powerful, then at very least a stern check on social frivolity. Now Philadelphia erupted with gaiety, with balls, entertainments, and gambling parties. Philadelphia had been the fountainhead and the capital of the new American nation; now, though by no means all Philadelphians forgot their devotion to the American cause, many Loyalists broke the silence in which they had been held by caution, uncertainty, or fear of reprisal; and there came out with them many who had leaned to the American side but thought that enough was enough, that rebellion had been attempted and had failed, and that the time had come to make a compromise peace. Many more who had no political opinions greeted the arrival of the British as a release from boredom. For the moment Philadelphia did its best to forget the Liberty Bell and the Continental Congress.

For all that, there was no great exultation among the Loyalists and none among the British officers whose attitude to life in Philadelphia was compounded of a natural relief at temporary end of battle against fellow citizens for whom they had no great hate and no less natural pleasure at exchanging the hardships of campaigning for the comforts of a civilized city, where the houses were warm, the larders well stocked, and the girls attractive.

Despite the presence not 10 miles away of American troops, despite occasional skirmishes and the undoubted activity within Philadelphia of many patriots who were passing to Washington every military rumor and every item of military intelligence that they could discover just as freely as a few weeks earlier when the Americans were in Philadelphia Loyalists had passed similar intelligence to Howe, Philadelphia was the most cheerful city in North America.

In such circumstances and in an army that regarded social accomplishment as a military qualification, few general officers were better suited than General Howe to command Philadelphia. Far away in Paris, Philadelphia's most prominent citizen grumbled "General Howe has not taken Philadelphia; Philadelphia has taken General Howe." The general stood six feet three tall, he was handsome, witty, a fine dancer, and unashamedly a ladies man. He enjoyed large dinner parties, and Philadelphia gave him many, with excellent food, fine French wines, and the company of well-dressed men and elegant women capable of conversation that came close to matching the standards of London or Bath. He loved to gamble for very high stakes and he found others in Philadelphia who shared this taste. He, like many of his officers and many Philadelphians, relished theatrical entertainments, but Philadelphia could not provide these for him unless the British army took upon itself the

General Sir William Howe. *Courtesy of The Historical Society of Pennsylvania.*

task of putting them on. For this important military operation Howe turned more and more often to the elegant young staff officer with artistic leanings: Captain John André.

Howe's delight in gaiety was not forced, and certainly André's collaboration in theatrical as in other pleasures was genuinely enthusiastic. But at their own levels of military service both Howe and André were officers above the ordinary, and their social energy would not have been so unrestrained had they not seen some advantage to their cause beyond the mere pursuit of pleasure. This was, indeed, a major exercise in propaganda. The general was intent on demonstrating to the Philadelphians how much better now was life with the British than it had been with their revolutionary countrymen, how much better indeed than it had ever been in the austere days of colonial provincialism before the war.

John André enjoyed Philadelphia, and Philadelphia loved John André. For an ardent soldier who had ambitions as an artist and as a poet, who enjoyed society, and reveled in the company of good-looking girls, what could be happier than life in a pleasure-loving city that was nevertheless close to the front. He could continue his intelligence work, write and produce plays, dine well with friends, and spend much time reading books borrowed from the excellent collection of the Library Company of Philadelphia or, with even greater ease, from the well-stocked shelves in the house where he was quartered—the house of Benjamin Franklin. For André, as for many another British officer, the greatest of all Philadelphia attractions was the beauty and charm of the Philadelphia girls. For André, and for such other British officers as could claim the privilege of their acquaintance, even in a city of lovelies there were none to equal the Shippen girls. And for André, among the three daughters of Edward Shippen, the youngest, Margaret, stood out as beyond doubt the prettiest and the most charming—so pretty and so charming that she drove from his mind any lingering sadness for his lost Honora.

Like so many of the leading families of Pennsylvania the Shippens were neither united nor consistent in their attitude to the great events that were going on around them. Peggy's grandfather served the revolutionary cause but, as we have seen, as a somewhat independent-minded official. Two uncles served in the Continental Army. Peggy's father, though he had held positions of some responsibility under the British and was generally thought to have Loyalist sympathies, seems to have been content to avoid all political commitment, offered his considerable hospitality to whichever side happened to occupy Philadelphia, and yet contrived to retain the respect of his neighbors. When the war was over, despite the disrepute brought to his family by Peggy, he was treated with honor by the new republic. All were Quakers, but this too did not keep them from entertaining on a large scale and certainly did not save Edward Shippen from spending vast sums on fashionable dresses for his daughters.

As for the daughters—a few young Philadelphian women might have dedicated themselves to one side or the other in the war, but the Shippen girls were obsessed with uniforms, and be they red or blue they did not much care.

To Peggy, at 17, John André in a uniform was the most handsome man that she had ever seen. But he was more. His conversation delighted her. She was flattered when he asked to be allowed to draw her portrait.

(Whether she, or André, realized that his artist's eye had seen more than his heart or mind could tell it is impossible to say, but certainly his picture of Peggy Shippen shows petulance as well as prettiness.) She was delighted when he took her to the plays that he had staged. But, despite her youth and her apparent frivolousness, Peggy Shippen was no fool. Others recognized in André qualities that made him stand out from among his contemporaries and even if she had not yet the perspicacity or the experience to see those qualities for herself, it is unthinkable that she would not have heard about them from her family, from her friends, and from his friends. Through André she was elevated into the company of men like Howe and Cornwallis whose greatness was not limited by the bounds of provincial society. One day, and that day soon, it seemed certain that André would be their equal. The prospect was dazzling to an ambitious 17-year-old girl who had never been outside Pennsylvania.

Whatever the two leading figures thought about their relationship—and that they thought about it a great deal is evident—the matchmakers saw marriage between John André and Peggy Shippen as a probability and no doubt were already planning a fine wedding that would outshine even the many elegant occasions held in Philadelphia during the British occupation.

But, if for the moment John André was the only man for Peggy Shippen, Peggy was certainly not the only girl for André. Another Peggy, the daughter of Chief Justice Benjamin Chew and a close friend of Peggy Shippen's, was also rumored to be about to announce her engagement to André. (Like Peggy Shippen, eventually she married an American general but even late in life was much given to recalling the charms of

Miss Margaret Shippen at 17 as drawn by John André. *Courtesy of Yale University Art Gallery.*

André, to the delight of listening friends and the fury of her husband who would interrupt her account with "He was nothing but a damned spy.") There was also Lydia Redman. If the evidence of some of André's verses can be taken as history, at least one Philadelphia girl had taken her romance with André beyond the limits that were acceptable in a Quaker city, though which one, whether Lydia Redman, Peggy Chew, Peggy Shippen, or some other, the classical convention of eighteenth-century verse must hold forever unrevealed.

It was, however, Peggy Chew who publicly deprived Peggy Shippen of what would have been her greatest social triumph, for it was Peggy Chew who wore André's favor in the greatest entertainment that Philadelphia had ever seen—probably the most lavish that it has ever known: the Mischianza which André organized as a farewell party for General Howe.

The popularity of General Howe, the enthusiasm and skill of John André as impresario, Philadelphian zest for entertainment—all these factors combined to make the Mischianza a happening of uninhibited sumptuousness. But, in the minds of those who planned and of those who looked forward excitedly to May 18, 1778, there was cause for rejoicing that, just because it was far more profound and entirely mistaken, was to make of this occasion in retrospect a bitter delusion. The British and the Loyalists imagined that they were to celebrate the virtual end of hostilities. Only a few months earlier, on October 13, 1777, the British had suffered their first major defeat of the war when General John Burgoyne had been forced to surrender at Saratoga, but since that date almost all military initiative had been with the British command. The Continental Army dwindled, as Washington himself complained, as much from the

neglect of their fellow Americans as from the hardships
of the climate or the depredation of their enemies.
Congress dwindled, like the army, so that at one time
there were only 20 representatives sitting at York.
Intercolony rivalries flared. There were plots to oust
Washington from his command. Accusations of
malpractice in administration were frequent—one
involved Peggy Shippen's uncle William.

On the other, the British side, Parliament was
preparing to concede to the Americans almost everything that they had asked for only three years earlier, and
a peace mission was on its way.

Against these considerations stood the implacability
of Washington himself and the splendid professionalism
of his drillmaster, von Steuben, but these alone would
not have held the American cause. Much more
significant, and indeed in the long run conclusive, was
the intervention of France.

The humiliations of the Seven Years War (in North
America known as the French and Indian Wars) had left
France with the determination to seek an early
opportunity to redress the balance of power. From the
outbreak of hostilities between the American colonies
and the mother country, the French government had
aided the American cause with money, arms, and
military advisers. But the French hesitated before
committing themselves unreservedly to an American
alliance, both because they had doubts about the
wisdom of encouraging republicanism and, more practi-
cally, because they had no wish to suffer at secondhand
yet another defeat by the British. Saratoga gave them
confidence, and so too did Britain's seeming reluctance
to conduct an all-out war. At the end of February 1778,
Franklin reported from Paris that:

> the most Christian King agrees to make common cause
> with the United States . . . and guarantees their
> liberty, sovereignty and independence

and when, in April, Washington heard of the treaty he wrote to Congress "I believe no event was ever received with more heartfelt joy." He knew that there would soon be at his side a regular army of considerable size and strength and the only navy that could battle effectively with Britain's Royal Navy would be immediately fighting in the American cause. He knew the renewal of spirit that the French alliance would breathe into shaky American hearts. He knew that Britain might soon find herself engaged on all the continents and all the oceans. If he had any qualms of conscience in accepting the aid of a despotic regime, with which for much of his previous military career he had been in conflict, those qualms he never whispered to his acquaintances.

The news of French intervention reached Philadelphia at about the same time as it reached George Washington. By then arrangements for the Mischianza were well advanced and nobody thought to call off the event. Indeed André, in this because of his Huguenot background even more easily blinded to the realities of international politics than were most of his colleagues, was convinced that the Alliance of the American cause with a Catholic and despotic regime would serve to encourage Loyalism among the Americans.

The Mischianza lasted for the whole of one day and one night. The war, politics, implications—all were forgotten. Those who took part and those who watched ignored the glowering displeasure of General Sir Henry Clinton, who had arrived from England to take over from Howe and who was known to regard this demonstration of adulation for his predecessor as in a sense an insult to himself and a rebuke to the government that had sent him out to replace the hero of the occasion, General Howe. Even, when in the early hours of the morning the sound of explosions was heard, the spectators were so delirious with pleasure that they accepted unquestioningly the explanation given them by British officers, that this was a part of the program. (The addition to the scenario was in fact accidentally devised by Captain Allan McLane of Philadelphia, an American cavalry officer, who with his dragoons was indulging in a hit-and-run attack on the British outposts.)

The party began with a water pageant. British generals, distinguished Philadelphians, male and female, young officers and their chosen ladies rowed up river in decorated barges, with bands playing and flags flying, until they were opposite Walnut Grove (the country mansion of the Wharton family) and disembarked and walked through files of soldiers to a place where a reconstruction of a jousting field had been laid out. There, with full panoply revived from medieval chivalry, seven Knights of the Blended Rose fought a bloodless battle with seven Knights of the Burning Mountain, while their chosen ladies, dressed for some reason in Turkish costume, sat watching from the seats of honor. André was one of the Knights of the Blended Rose; his device, two gamecocks fighting, his motto "No Rival," and his lady, Peggy Chew. According to one account Peggy Shippen, though displaced as André's favorite, was one of the ladies of the Blended Rose; her knight, Lieutenant Sloper. By another account the Turkish costume designed for her by André was too daring even for the easy going Edward Shippen and Peggy was forbidden from taking part. According to protests that were later raised loudly and frequently by the Shippens, Peggy and her sisters were not even present at Walnut Grove, but by the time these protests were made the winds of fortune had changed direction and participation in the Mischianza had become a measure of disloyalty to the American cause.

After the jousting there followed dancing, gambling, eating, and drinking. There were bars on every floor of Walnut Grove, each of them richly decorated and transformed by André's ingenuity from its pristine eighteenth-century elegance into some outlandish mode. The gambling room was decorated in what André took to be the style of ancient Egypt. General Sir William Howe and his brother Admiral Richard Howe led to supper the procession of 430 guests. And after supper there was more dancing, more drinking, more gambling, and finally, at four in the morning, a fireworks display.

Less than three weeks later General Clinton received orders to abandon Philadelphia and to concentrate on New York. All previous successes were thus thrown away, and Clinton's army, making its way overland, found itself fighting desperate rearguard actions and might well have been destroyed had it not been for the indecisiveness of one of Washington's generals, another former British army officer, Charles Lee. Some 3,000 Loyalists were moved by sea from Philadelphia to New York. The Shippens were not among their number.

Clinton had completed the evacuation of Philadelphia on June 18, 1778. Next day the city was occupied by the Americans under Major General Benedict Arnold. Within weeks Arnold had met Peggy Shippen and by September he was offering her marriage.

André's unbridled demonstration of enthusiasm for General Howe could well have caused him some embarrassment with Howe's successor, but Clinton seemed no less determined than Howe to secure the advancement of the young officer and no less eager to number him among his personal friends. André was made one of two commissioners entrusted with the task of negotiating with the Americans over the conditions of prisoners of war. When General Grey returned to England, Clinton had André appointed to his own staff, and it was as Clinton's personal representative that André received the surrender of Fort Lafayette. And in September 1779 Clinton made André deputy adjutant-general.

As there was no adjutant-general in North America, André was placed in effect at the head of his part of the military service. It was a remarkable achievement for an officer who had served for only eight years, who had started without friends or money, and who had bought only one step in his promotion: the majoity in the 54th Regiment (later the Dorsets) which went with his appointment as deputy adjutant-general. But André never allowed his punctilious performance of his military duties to interfere with his artistic and social activities. In New York André was billeted at Clinton's out-of-town residence, close to the point where now 51st Street touches First Avenue. (The general's headquarters was at No. 1 Broadway.) From there he organized not only the administration and the intelligence of the British army but also the production of plays. He gave a witty lecture "On love and fashion." He continued to write verse. He indulged in several flirtations. Very soon he was in correspondence with some of his old Philadelphia friends, among them Peggy Shippen.

Ostensibly the subject of these letters was no more sinister than an offer to smuggle finery for the ladies such as they could no longer buy in Philadelphia. But on April 8, 1779, Peggy Shippen had become Mrs. Benedict Arnold.

Already the British authorities were aware that Arnold was restless, dissatisfied, a potential turncoat. André's letters to Peggy Shippen may have been no more than a gallant and sentimental gesture but, if so, the coincidence is remarkable. It is far more likely that André was attempting to construct a means of communication with the brave, flamboyant, and erratic American general, Benedict Arnold.

3. Benedict Arnold

FOR ALL HIS sensitivity John André was a dedicated and professional staff officer. His courage was indisputable but so was his realism. From his own experience and from the heritage of his craft, he knew a great deal about the contradictory nature of war, how it can change from being a well-nigh impersonal and essentially intellectual exercise in strategy, intelligence, and tactics and become, without warning, a desperately personal and lonely adventure in which the individual looks straight into the eyes of death. Like every soldier in every war André had suffered premonitions, clear minded only in the knowledge that today would be his last. But, like most soldiers, he had also known that many of his companions had shared these premonitions and that most of them had lived to talk about them.

But, as he felt his way toward encouraging Arnold into treachery, André had no premonition of disaster. This, for him was a routine affair, exciting only insofar as Arnold was the most important among several Americans whose loyalty to the American cause it was his duty to test and, if possible, to subvert. Failure to secure Arnold's treason would be disappointing but in no way personally dangerous. That there could be any risk to his own safety was, at least at the beginning of the affair, unthinkable just because there was in fact no risk.

For Arnold the case was different. For him it was all risk, risk that he might be discovered, risk that, for some reason that he could not envisage, he might be betrayed by those he was proposing to serve, risk that, even if his treachery was fulfilled, those to whom he deserted might not live by their promises.

But Arnold was a gambler on a scale that would have shaken André's friends in the Egyptian room at Walnut Grove. His career had been made by staking his own life and reputation, and on several occasions he had almost lost the one grand stake or the other.

Benedict Arnold was born at Norwich, Connecticut, on February 14, 1741, the son of another Benedict, a sea captain and merchant whose voyaging and mercantile prosperity were both ended by his pleasure in the bottle. The Arnolds and Benedict's mother's family, the Kings, were long-established New England families of the middle sort, seldom prominent but never humble.

In this, unlike André, Arnold's subsequent disastrous career awakened reminiscence of many of his boyhood companions, and the record is full of tales of his youthful callousness, bad temper, and even cruelty; so full, indeed, that it is likely that most of the stories were written in hindsight to demonstrate the foresight of the storyteller.

One criticism of Arnold, that he was uneducated, was circulated early in his public career, was underlined at the time of his treachery, and has lingered on to this day in the Arnold fable. But it was an invention of his critics and enemies and by implication of a justification of the American cause, as if to say that only a boor could fail to understand the eternal righteousness of the Revolution. By the standards of his time, Arnold was well educated, first by Dr. Jewett at a school in

Montville, Connecticut, and then from the age of 11 by the Reverend James Cogswell at Canterbury, 14 miles from Norwich. Hannah Arnold sent her son to Cogswell with strict instructions that the schoolmaster should not spoil the child by sparing his rod. This, too, has been taken as an indication that the boy was notably unruly, though such instructions were commonplace in the eighteenth century even from the parents of the best behaved children and were but extensions into the school of the manner in which even the most loving parents brought up both sons and daughters. The advice was almost certainly redundant. Under Cogswell's austere tuition and ready rod Arnold became a competent Latinist and more than ordinarily skillful at arithmetic. Under Mrs. Cogswell's careful eye he was trained to be tidy, but neither Mr. Cogswell nor his wife could break Benedict's habit of substituting a loud voice for quiet and graceful argument.

When Arnold was 14, financial disaster hit his family. He was taken away from school and for a while allowed to exercise without restraint his zest for swimming, sailing, and brawling. He was soon in trouble with the authorities who were prepared to ignore his escapades so long as they involved only his contemporaries but could not accept as just boyish enthusiasm an offer to fight the town constable. In the hope of achieving for her son both immediate discipline and a future career that could be stimulating and profitable, Hannah Arnold apprenticed him to her cousins, the Lathrop brothers, apothecaries of Norwich. Theirs was no mere local druggists' business, for the Lathrops imported many kinds of goods from Britain and even from the East Indies, and at the outbreak of the French and Indian Wars won the contract for supplying surgical equipment to the army in the Lake George area. Arnold, who was soon to show a good head for trade and a keen interest in profit, might well have settled comfortably enough in a business that was not without romance and excitement had not his initiation coincided with events that offered adventures far more glorious than anything that could come from an apothecary's shop.

From 1754, the year before Arnold left Dr. Cogswell's, the frontier had been alight. A young Virginian officer, George Washington, out on a mission that combined exploration, diplomatic endeavor, and military effort in western Maryland and Pennsylvania, blundered into a French and Indian stronghold at Great Meadows (near the town now called Confluence) and was forced to surrender. Two regiments of regulars under General Edward Braddock, with the same George Washington as staff officer, were routed by the French near Fort Duquesne (now Pittsburgh, Pennsylvania). The French and their Indian allies threatened the safety of all the American colonies, the British seemed incapable of mastering the techniques of North American warfare, and each of the colonial governments seemed content to look only to the safety of its own frontiers and to the dignity of its own independence from any military interference from any other colonial government.

But this was a time of crisis, and crisis itself was exciting to young Arnold. And then in 1756 war between Britain and France became complete and virtually worldwide. A patriotism richer than loyalty to the colony gripped British Americans, among them Benedict Arnold. The editor of the *Pennsylvania Gazette*, Benjamin Franklin, urged the colonies to "Join or Die," and in London in June 1757, the new Secretary of State for War William Pitt, set to work planning the grand strategy which (against all odds) would win for Britain an empire in India and expel the French from Canada. There were new heroes whose names were as familiar in Norwich, Connecticut, as they were in London: Boscawen, Hawke, Wolfe, Eyre Coote, and Clive.

It was no time to be an apothecary's apprentice. In March 1758 Arnold ran away from home, crossed the border into New York (where the bounty for enlistment was higher) and joined the militia. Within weeks he was back in the Norwich shop, humiliatingly mustered out at the request of his mother, and in that year when Louisbourg was taken by James Wolfe, when the French lost control of Lake Ontario, when they were driven out of the Ohio Valley and when their great fortress at Fort Duquesne was recaptured and renamed, after the architect of victory, Pittsburgh, Arnold fumed and fretted in Norwich.

For the British and the British Americans, if not for Benedict Arnold, 1758 was marvellous, but 1759 was the great year of victories, and this time Arnold had his chance of a humble share in the glory. In the first months of the year there was a much publicized call for volunteers, and Arnold managed to persuade his mother that he should go. Once more he preferred the New York bounty.

In August 1759 Admiral Boscawen destroyed a French fleet off the coast of Portugal. On September 13 the British captured Quebec in an action that killed both hero commanders, Wolfe and the French general Montcalm. In November, Admiral Hawke destroyed the French Fleet in the English Channel. "We are forced to ask every morning what victory there is," wrote Horace Walpole, "for fear of missing one." But in all that "wonderful year" the only fame that came to Benedict Arnold was an advertisement in a New York paper offering 40 shillings for his arrest as a deserter. Arnold had wanted to fight; instead, he found himself drilling. He hoped to perform great acts of valor; instead, they forced him to clear forests. He had, too, one good reason for changing his mind about military service: his mother was seriously ill. She died in August, and with her death Arnold lost the only stable influence that he ever knew.

Arnold returned to the colors in 1760, his act of desertion apparently forgotten and forgiven; but by then the war in North America was virtually over and he was soon demobilized, behind him three short, unsatisfactory periods as a soldier and not the echo of a shot in his memory.

Norwich, without his mother and without any military exploits to boast about to his stay-at-home friends, was no longer for him; and the place became unbearable when his father was arrested for drunkenness. For a while Arnold was shiftless. He sailed as a supercargo on a ship for the West Indies. He worked in Middletown, Hartford, and even in England. When his father died in 1761 Arnold settled in New Haven.

With his share of the proceeds from the sale of their family home he set himself up as "B. Arnold, Druggist, Bookseller, & c. from London." The *etcetera* was truly all embracing. Arnold sold spices, fruit, wines, paints, watches, jewelery, maps, pictures, tea, sugar, and rum as well as "many other Articles, very cheap, for Cash or short Credit." As for his proclaimed trades: the druggist stocked among other things "Essence Balm Gilead" and "Pectoral Balsam Honey," the bookseller, the ancient classics, modern novels, "Hillary on the Small Pox" and "West and Littleton on the Resurrection."

In New Haven he was soon joined by his sister Hannah who adored him even though he had driven off her principal suitor with a pistol shot just because the man was a Frenchman and a Catholic—two failings in a human being that Arnold would always find unforgivable.

The business prospered and Arnold spent less and less time in New Haven and more and more time in traveling to Canada and on his own ships to the West Indies. With his profits, so did his reputation for explosive violence grow, and as relations deteriorated between the New England merchants and the British government, Arnold came to be regarded as a leader of the wilder sort who preferred abusive words and ruthless actions to negotiation.

In activities of this kind Arnold found compensation for the active-service soldiering that he had missed and he soon discovered that a New England merchant who was prepared to flout laws made in London and ready and able to support his independence with deed and word could establish for himself a reputation among like-minded neighbors that was no less dashing than fame won on a battlefield. The times were ripe for action.

Almost from the beginning of American colonization there had been tensions between British trading interests and the aspirations of colonial merchants. British imperial policy was founded on the principle that the colonies should produce raw materials and rely for the most part on Britain for manufactured goods and services. Much parliamentary legislation about the colonies was designed to foster this division of activity and almost all of it had been unpopular in the colonies, particularly in New England, and above all among New

England shipowners whose only substantial hope of success lay in direct competition with their British-based counterparts. Opposition to, circumvention of, the law became part of the New England way of life, and hardheaded Yankee merchants refused to regard even the circumstances of the Seven Years War as sufficient reason for giving up their lucrative trade with the French West Indies. During that war, Britain had been too busy to enforce the regulations, but with the war won and Britain well-nigh bankrupted (as the British saw it, in part because they had saved the colonials from the French and the Indians), Parliament determined to strengthen and increase the restrictions, and at the same time to force the Americans to foot part of the bill for their own defense.

Customs regulations were tightened, customs posts reinforced; in American waters the Royal Navy became virtually a revenue patrol; informers were encouraged, and colonial judges freed from dependence upon colonial assemblies.

For many New England merchants evasion of the Acts of Trade and Navigation became a patriotic duty and smuggling a noble profession. Arnold's "patriotism" was open, noisy, and ruthless. Argument and even illicit trading were not enough for him. Though he joined with many of his New England colleagues in frequent public outbursts against the Acts as infringements of "the rights of Englishmen," though with them he sailed and traded in ways that were specifically forbidden by the Acts, he went further than all but a very few by introducing violence into the vocabulary of opposition. On one occasion, for example, he led a party of vigilantes, dragged from a tavern one of his own sailors, Peter Boles (admittedly a blackmailer as well as an informer), and gave the man 40 lashes at a public whippingpost. This ruthless behavior shocked even the citizens of New Haven. Arnold was tried and fined 50 shillings, but he was not contrite; instead he attacked his judges in the local newspaper:

> Is it good policy or would so great a number of people, in any trading town of the continent (New Haven excepted) vindicate, caress, and protect an informer?

Arnold's air of self-righteous indignation might have been more convincing had his tough lawlessness been confined to episodes which could be justified by the unfairness of Parliament, but on several other occasions Arnold had revealed the hastiness and violence of his nature in quarrels of an entirely personal nature in which he was generally more sinner than sinned against; quarrels that led to duels which invariably he won. Nevertheless, his appeal to public opinion over the Boles affair was well timed. The day of the moderate was drawing to a close.

There were, however, problems pressing on Arnold, as on many of his New England neighbors, that could not be solved with a bitter speech, an angry letter to the press, or even a knotted rope. His credit was already overstretched, and in the recession of 1767 it came close to snapping. He tried some quick financial footwork which, though it was illegal, was for all that no more dishonest than that practiced by many an outwardly respectable Yankee merchant, and just managed to save his business.

Despite temporary setbacks Arnold could be well pleased with the progress that he had made. In only eight years the one-time deserter had become a leading citizen of New Haven, locally famous for his forthrightness, his business energy, his temper, his elegant dress, and for his skill as an athlete. His presence was notable, and the promise for his future obviously great and made all the more auspicious when, on February 22, 1767, he married Margaret Mansfield, daughter of the high sheriff of the county and a member of one of the wealthiest and most socially acceptable families of New Haven.

Peggy Mansfield Arnold was three years younger than her husband and in almost everything unlike him. Quiet, fragile, inclined to piety, she adored her rumbustious husband; and for his part Arnold treated her with a gentleness that was foreign to his nature (and not always present in his relations with his second wife). But marriage exaggerated one trait which, already obvious in Arnold, was in the future to contribute substantially to his difficulties: his love of ostentation. Determined to show the world that he had arrived and eager to represent to his well-bred wife the measure of his love for her, he showered her with luxuries and surrounded her with grandeurs such as even her prosperous father had not been able to provide for her. From 1767 on, although at times Arnold was a very rich man, he lived always beyond his means.

The most grandiose of his many expensive gifts to Peggy, and for Arnold himself the greatest and most public demonstration of his established eminence in New Haven, was the estate that he began to plan as soon as their first child (another Benedict) was born in February 1768, and then began to build after the birth of Richard in August 1769; he then occupied the estate just before the arrival of their third son, Henry, in September 1772.

The house itself was handsome, well built, and

handsomely furnished. By New Haven standards it was large but what made it exceptional was the site—three acres overlooking the harbor and the sound, the elaborate gardens, and its immediate proximity to Arnold's own wharves and his new store.

Marriage, a family, and a new home did not quieten Arnold's manner, diminish his arrogance, or even keep him in New Haven. Indeed, his journeys to Canada and to the West Indies became more frequent and longer, and his explosive behavior and his vaunted success made him enemies both among the quieter townsfolk and among those who were jealous of his business skill.

But the political climate in Connecticut, as in the other colonies, was becoming more and more comfortable for men of Arnold's disposition; and those of a quieter sort were discovering that their pacific or accommodating nature could bring down upon them not merely accusations of disloyalty to the American cause but even physical retribution. Increasingly the debate over trade was being submerged by more bitter quarrels about representation, taxation, and the authority of a distant Parliament. Still, American orators thumped out the demand that they be allowed to enjoy their rights as freeborn Englishmen, but now some of them preached the need to defend those rights "in battle and blood," and in New Haven the most eager and, as always, the noisiest of the radicals was Benedict Arnold.

On March 5, 1770, in Boston a small force of regular troops fired on a mob of toughs. John Adams undertook the defense of the soldiers when they were tried before a civil court. Most of the evidence was on his side and the military were exonerated; but John Adams' cousin, Sam, now had a rallying cry, "Remember the Boston Massacre!" for those who would accept no compromise.

From then on with increasing vigor American opinion began to respond to the call. Arnold, for one, did not hesitate. When the news of the "Boston Massacre" reached him in the West Indies he erupted in a letter which for all its apparent devotion to the cause of freedom seems to reveal delight that force could now be justified:

> Good God! Are the Americans all asleep and calmly giving up their glorious liberty . . . that they don't take immediate vengeance on such miscreants?

War was not yet inevitable, and Arnold had to wait for three years, fuming with impatience, before he could become a vehicle for the vengeance he urged; but increasingly his name was associated with those who worked to incite rebellion, to organize Americans for the war that they hoped would come, and to terrorize those who were not of their opinion.

The follies of the British government and the hopelessness of compromise brought many even among moderate-minded colonials to the view that war was their only hope. But New Haven was, when compared to other New England towns, slow to settle itself in a military stance. At last in December 1774, 65 "gentlemen of influence and high respectability" formed themselves into a military group. Arnold was one of the 65. In February 1775 the group set up a committee of three to investigate the purchase of arms. Arnold was one of the three. On March 2, 1775, the group petitioned the Connecticut General Assembly for a charter as the Governor's Second Company of guards. (The First Company had been formed in Hartford as long ago as 1771.) Arnold was named as commander.

His true career had begun.

His nomination as captain of the Guards was a tribute to his personality, to his potentiality as a leader, and to his harshly acquired social acceptability. But for him this appointment brought to the surface ambitions that had never been deeply submerged. His patriotic fervor cannot be doubted but it was equalled by his pride and pleasure in the profession to which he had at last been called. Soldiering offered to him opportunities for adventure unequalled by any civil occupation. As a soldier his explosiveness could be transformed into boldness, his zest for violence nobly translated into bravery, his habitual arrogance usefully exploited as decisiveness. Even, and it was to him by no means a frivolous consideration, his love of personal finery could be exercised handsomely, for no civilian dress could compete with the extravagant uniform of an eighteenth-century officer. (Arnold and his Guards wore scarlet tunics faced with buff, ruffled shirts, white vests, and breeches and black leggings.)

Even now, though sumptuously uniformed and armed with local authority the chances of Arnold establishing himself as a fighting soldier seemed slight indeed. In most of the colonies men were forming military associations like the Connecticut Guards. In some these militiamen seized stocks of arms and ammunition. The royal colonial governments were in disarray and in their place sat provincial assemblies. But even as they girded themselves for action many in America looked hopefully for news from England where, as was well known among Americans, two magnificent statesmen, the Earl of Chatham (William Pitt, the Elder, hero of the Seven Years War) and Edmund Burke, were conducting in and out of Parliament a great campaign to bring about conciliation.

Only in Massachusetts were American preparations for war wholehearted and well organized. But it was also only in Massachusetts that the British had a military force of strength sufficient to quell an uprising—the army under General Gage quartered on Boston. There, in Massachusetts, flint and steel were too close for safety. On April 19, 1775, the spark was struck. The conciliations had failed, Gage had received orders to use force to bring the Americans back to their dutiful senses and to arrest the more rabid American leaders, among them Sam Adams. Gage moved a small detachment from Boston toward Concord. At Lexington they faced armed Americans. Someone fired a shot, then more shots. The British withdrew to Boston and the American Revolution had begun.

It was still, in a sense, a fight between Massachusetts and Britain. In other colonies the majority applauded the actions of the heroes of Lexington and argued as to just how much or just how little military support should be given to the Massachusetts forces suddenly thrust into the surprising role of besieging Boston, General Gage, and the only substantial British force in North America. Lexington had given new inspiration to the will to resist; it had not persuaded Americans to an entire commitment to a unified cause. Echoes of the first shot at Lexington, the shot that was later said to have been heard around the world, were heard in New Haven two days later. Immediately a town meeting was called to decide the measure of support for Massachusetts. The radicals managed to get their own man elected chairman but only by one vote, and they could not persuade a majority to favor aid for Massachusetts. New Haven's militia must stay at home to guard the safety of New Haven.

Benedict Arnold would not be hindered. He gathered together his Guards and bustled them into a decision to march on the very next day to Massachusetts.

Next morning the Guards, their numbers swelled by volunteers from Yale, assembled for inspection by Captain Arnold. Splendidly clothed, well armed, and (presumably with the exception of the Yale novices) well versed in the drill manual, they prepared to march off behind their colors. But one important item was missing from their equipment: they had no powder or shot, and the New Haven ammunition store was under the control of the very men who had refused to send troops to Massachusetts. Not surprisingly they also refused Arnold's polite request for military supplies, and Arnold's politeness vanished. He would have powder and shot even if he had to see to it that first battle honor on the colors of the Second Company of Guards was a successful assault on the New Haven magazine. The committeemen sent a mediator. If only Arnold would show patience then the civic leaders might, indeed undoubtedly would, change their minds, and the Guards would receive orders to march from a properly constituted authority.

Arnold snapped out his reply: "None but Almighty God shall prevent my marching." The peacemaker hurried back to the city fathers with the sad news that the Almighty was not likely to prove much of an ally and that Arnold and his men were showing signs that they were not willing to wait for a fight until they met British soldiers. Within minutes Arnold's company was fully equipped and on the road to Cambridge where the colonial militia was gathering.

Arnold had won his first military engagement. Just

by raising his voice at the right moment he had defeated his fellow townsfolk. But, once he reached Cambridge and saw the anthology of independent units from many colonies which formed the force besieging Boston, he soon came to realize that there were present many others with voices just as loud as his, whose experience was far greater, and who had behind them support more weighty and more assured than he was likely to receive from New Haven and Connecticut. If he were to serve the American cause, as he knew himself to be capable of serving, as a powerful and energetic commander, he must draw attention to himself, and he must look for preferment where real power still lay, with the Massachusetts' authorities.

His opportunity he recognized immediately. The forces around Boston were short of artillery. From his earlier travels Arnold remembered that there was a considerable store of British cannon and only a small detachment of British troops at Fort Ticonderoga. He put a plan to the Massachusetts Committee of Safety for the capture of fort, cannon, and troops. His personality was so powerful, his plan so bold, and their need of cannon so great, that the committee promptly posted him as colonel, gave him a little money, the authority to raise volunteers for the exploit, and orders to move on Ticonderoga.

Unfortunately for Arnold, the need for artillery and the chance of filling that need at Ticonderoga were as obvious to others as to him; and, before he began to move, several detachments, including one from his native Connecticut and another from Massachusetts, the newly acquired source of his own authority, were already set for the same goal. From Arnold's point of view worst of all, the strongest force was commanded by

Ethan Allen, an officer who could outdo even Arnold as a swashbuckler. Most of Allen's Green Mountain Boys came from Vermont (which as yet had no recognized revolutionary government) and in the muddled and undignified squabble over command which followed, Allen's supremacy was upheld by Connecticut and tacitly by New York, whose territory included Ticonderoga. An uneasy duality of command was contrived, but for all except Arnold there was little doubt that Allen was the first of two equals. Even the British officer at Ticonderoga recognized the situation. When his 40 men were caught asleep, he put on his dressing gown, sent for his sword, and handed it to Allen. Arnold complained to the Massachusetts' authorities that Allen "positively insisted that I should have no command, as I had forbidden the soldiers plundering and destroying private property." Arnold had seized a small ship, the private property of one of the local residents, sailed it up Lake Champlain to the Canadian end, and captured a British post even smaller than Ticonderoga (and far less useful).

Months passed before the cannon from Ticonderoga reached Cambridge, but the news of the exploit spread throughout the colonies, and always the hero's part was given to Allen. Arnold, who had hoped for glory, soon found himself faced instead with the possibility of ignominy. Those who had given him authority, their ears filled with reports of his querulous behavior, ordered him to accept Allen's seniority. Arnold refused. If Massachusetts doubted his rectitude and abilities, this "is sufficient inducement for me to decline serving them longer." To the reports that were justified were added wilder rumors. It was said that Arnold had incited his men to mutiny and even that he had threatened to take them over to the British. An investigating committee was sent from Cambridge to Ticonderoga and summed up its opinion with the evasive comment that "the particulars were too tedious and disagreeable to report." Even so, the air was thick with recriminations. Arnold claimed that he had never received the money he had been promised for the expedition and that he had mortgaged considerable private funds to its support; his enemies accused him of embezzling funds, and even those who were not against him were forced to admit that he had been so eager for action and command that he had not had time to keep proper accounts. He was ordered back to Cambridge to undergo a full-scale investigation. Arnold resigned his commission and disbanded his troops.

Full of bitterness against Massachusetts, his fellow officers, and fate, Arnold made his way slowly to Albany and there received news of a decision that might have heartened him for it promised an end to the dissension, rivalries, lack of cooperation and political maneuvring among the colonies which had contributed to his downfall. On June 15 the Continental Congress meeting in Philadelphia had resolved that "a General be appointed to command all the Continental forces raised for the defense of American liberty." On the same day "George Washington Esq. was unanimously elected."

But any comfort that Arnold might have gathered from consideration of this decision was submerged by other and more intimate news waiting for him at Albany. On June 19 his wife had died. Fate, it seemed, would permit to him neither glory on the battlefield nor the quiet of comfortable married life.

He struggled back to New Haven and for a while it seemed as if the fires of ambition had died with Peggy. Dutifully, he discussed with his sister the future of his three small children and set about restoring his battered business affairs. But he had no spirit for war and none even for cantankerous letter writing. Then, as if physically shaking himelf free from the burdens of injustice and tragedy, Arnold came to life again. Hannah was quite capable of caring for the business and for the daily life of his children. The best that he could do to secure a glorious future for his family was to ensure his own future glory. As he had to answer the criticisms from Massachusetts, then for that too the unshakable response would be, not a clerk's defense to the accusations of clerks about past events (though a defense he was certain he could provide) but some immediate and sensational victory that would prove his patriotism, his gallantry, and his soldierly superiority over those who had dared to doubt both his motives and his skills as a commander.

From his trading experience he knew the Canadian border better than most and he had added to his knowledge with his recent campaigning. He drafted a proposal for an invasion of Canada.

As with the Ticonderoga exploit many others had similar dreams and several had put them to paper. Americans were shrewdly aware of the strategic importance of Fort George, Montreal, and, more particularly, Quebec, which stood as the very symbol of Britain's recently acquired northern dominions. They were less shrewd when they made the assumption that they had only to invade Canada to bring to their side both French and English Canadians. But in pursuit of both strategic and political aims, Congress ordered two armies into Canada. The one, under the command of General Schuyler (soon to be replaced by General Montgomery), was to take the Champlain—Sorel route against Montreal and would then move toward Quebec there to join with the second force that had come up by a far more hazardous route—through the wilderness by way of the Chaudière, the Dead, and Kennebec rivers. The command of this right-hook assault Washington gave to Arnold. It was, in some ways, a fantastic decision. Arnold stood on the brink of disgrace. His Canadian experience did not include any knowledge of the route he was to take. (Indeed, no one except the Indians and, in 1761, one British officer had ever used the wilderness route.) Arnold's previous military exploits had made him famous only for insubordination. Washington recognized that what he offered was no command for a conventional soldier. Those rumbustious attributes which had brought Arnold into disfavor might well prove to be assets beyond price in the wilderness. Possibly Washington already recognized that Arnold would have to be used somewhere and that if he served close to the center of affairs he would soon be involved in new quarrels. It is likely that he felt for Arnold in his bereavement. It is conceivable that Washington, who in the past had himself suffered from the petty mindedness of provincial authorities, shared Arnold's conviction that a successful exploit would be the one truly satisfactory reply to Arnold's critics.

Whatever Washington's reasons, his choice was proved undeniably sound. In all his career as a commander in the Revolution, Arnold never showed himself so assuredly a leader of men as he did in the fall of 1775.

The wilderness march was more a journey of exploration than a military expedition with the difference that when it was completed Arnold had to produce his men ready to launch an assault against one of the great fortresses of North America. Arnold drove his men through swamp and forest, along rivers and over portages. They ran out of food and survived by eating dogs, boiled moccasins, and gruel made from shaving soap. They waded through icy streams, built rafts, shot rapids, and hacked paths where no paths had ever been. Many deserted and, as usual with Arnold, some of his senior officers took such strenuous exception to his methods of command that they proposed his replacement. But, though his stocky form shrank, the light in his eyes seemed to grow ever brighter, and the authority in his voice grew ever firmer.

On November 8, 1775, Arnold and his exhausted and much depleted force reached Levis opposite Quebec. (Two weeks earlier the other army invading Canada under Montgomery had captured Fort Chambly and a young British officer, John André.)

Now Arnold's good fortune began to run out but not his ambition or his courage. The French Canadian peasants did not heed the prophesies of Congress and rise in support of an American army; the French Canadian aristocracy and townspeople stayed loyal to the British. Intelligence reports from within Quebec exaggerated the size of the British garrison and led Arnold to believe that his tiny force was greatly outnumbered. Still, there stood Quebec, the prize won for Britain by the hero of Arnold's youth, James Wolfe, and Arnold knew that if he captured the city he would be acclaimed by his countrymen not merely as Wolfe's equal but also as the first substantial victor in a cause far nobler than Wolfe's. Following Wolfe's tactical example, Arnold crossed the St. Lawrence, landed at Anse au Foulon, and scaled the heights of Abraham. But there the similarity between Arnold and his great British predecessor ended. The British commander also remem-

bered Wolfe and refused to make the same mistake that
Montcalm had made in 1759. However much Arnold
probed and taunted, he refused to be lured out to do
battle on the Plains of Abraham. Nor would he
surrender. Now for the first time in his career Arnold
showed himself to be something more than a dashing
and determined leader of men. Though disappointed
and frustrated of immediate victory and consequent
long-term glory, he proved himself to be a true general.
He determined to blockade Quebec and, even though
this would make him once more a second-in-command,
to wait for the arrival of Montgomery and his army
before attacking Quebec.

Arnold was not given to quick forgiveness of those
whom he thought had wronged him; and when he heard
from Montreal that Ethan Allen had been captured in a
mad and unnecessary assault on a position which was
virtually impregnable, he must have received the news
with some sardonic pleasure.

The next important report from Montreal was good
by any standards that an American general could apply.
Carleton, like Montcalm in 1759, realizing the impossi-
bility of his position, had abandoned Montreal and was
making for Quebec by river.

Parenthetically, it is both interesting and significant
(and may be also surprising to those who think of
"armies" in twentieth-century terms) that the forces
engaged on both sides in the Canadian campaigns of
1775 were tiny. Montgomery, commanding the main
invasion army, had at his disposal only 1,500 men,
Arnold never more than 1,000. The British had 400
troops in Quebec. The "army" which Carleton was now
attempting to bring from Montreal to Quebec was 130
strong!

From now on the French Canadian militia stood to

arms with a will beside their British colleagues. Arnold
had not lost to Montgomery his chance to be the
"liberator of Canada"; that chance had been taken from
them both by Carleton and the Canadians.

Still the Americans hoped; and now, with Montgomery as his superior, Arnold showed a side of his
character as a soldier that was revealed only when he
served with the very few officers who won his unstinted
admiration. He became an excellent second-in-command. He recognized that Montgomery's courage was
equal to his own and Montgomery's experience much
greater. He liked the general's manner and his tact, but
he also admired Montgomery's firm discipline—a seemingly paradoxical concession from a man so often hot
with anger against authority. The contradiction is
reduced when one remembers Arnold's martinet drilling
of the New Haven Guards and disappears altogether
before consideration that the combination of tact and
stern discipline was one attribute that Arnold himself
could never acquire. He admired it all the more when he
saw it successfully exercised by others.

However, as the Americans shivered in the bitter
Canadian winter, their numbers depleted by frostbite,
smallpox, and desertion, tempers frayed and Arnold
gathered to himself a new pack of enemies who were to
snap at his heels for months and some of them for years
to come.

Tactically, Arnold was ready. He placed his ambush
at exactly the right place and captured Carleton's little
flotilla. But it was an incomplete victory. In a manner
which Arnold would not have been ashamed to imitate,
Carleton saw as his principal duty the need to get himself
to Quebec to take over command there. Disguised as a
Canadian farmer, he made his way through Arnold's

lines and reached the beleaguered fortress. By the time
that Montgomery and Arnold joined forces they were
faced by the wisest British commander in North
America. From their point of view even worse (though
the Americans did not yet know it), the seemingly
miraculous arrival in Quebec of a British general who
had always shown himself well disposed toward the
French Canadians removed from French Canadian
minds any lingering hesitancy that they might have felt
about defending the British Empire.

Carleton, his men housed comfortably in Quebec,
and, though their numbers were still not large, sheltered
by heavy artillery, turned away with disdain every
invitation to surrender. Montgomery, well aware of the
difficulties and dangers of a frontal attack against a
fortified position, decided nonetheless that "to the
storming we must come at last." Arnold agreed with him
wholeheartedly, but their views were not shared by many
under them and seemed particularly obnoxious to those,
both officers and men, whose enlistment period was due
to end on January 1, 1776. The battlefield is no place for
democratic institutions, but the Americans had not yet
outgrown their small-town customs. If not all ranks,
then certainly all officers demanded the right to discuss
in council and to vote on every major decision. Many
voted against an attack on Quebec, and just as Arnold
was the most vocal of those who spoke up for the assault
so were most of those who opposed the notion ostensibly
his men.

Montgomery's opinion and Arnold's voice won the
debate but, by implication at least, notice had been
served that, if the assault failed, the blame would be set
to Arnold's account.

The assault did fail. Indeed, the Battle of Quebec,

fought on the last day of 1775, was in military terms probably, and in political consequences certainly, the most catastrophic battle ever fought by the armies of the American Revolution. American deserters told Carleton that the assault was coming, and he placed his men with immaculate care. Montgomery attacked from the direction of Wolfe's Cove, Arnold through St. Roque. Both forces were met with devastating fire. Montgomery, so recently a British officer, was killed by the first shot from a muzzle-loader manned by Royal Navy gunners. Arnold, at the head of a small advance party, was wounded in the left leg, fainted from loss of blood, and had to be carried out of the danger zone. At the end of a short, sharp battle from an American attacking force of about 800, 48 were dead (including a high proportion of senior officers), 34 were wounded, and 372 captured. At least 100 promptly deserted. The defenders had lost 12 dead and 30 wounded.

For months Arnold, though in great pain, continued the siege of Quebec. A new commander, David Wooster, took over in Montreal where he was soon joined by a mighty figure, Benjamin Franklin, who was charged with two tasks: the first, to win with words what bullets had failed to achieve—the accession of a fourteenth colony, Canada, to the Revolutionary cause; the second, as ever, to investigate the conduct of American officers, which meant, once more, an investigation of Arnold's relations with his subordinates. There was some consolation for Arnold. He was promoted to brigadier general and told that he had been appointed to the command of one of the new Continental regiments now being raised by order of Congress. Washington congratulated him on his courageous and skillful endeavors.

There were still battles to fight in Canada, and Congress ordered substantial reinforcements to the north. By March 1776 Arnold was ready to fight again; but experience, promotion, and congratulations did not deflect the unalterable rules of seniority. There were now no less than three officers in Canada who outranked him and not one a man of the Montgomery pattern. Arnold quarreled with each of them in turn; and those under his command who had come to dislike him even before the Battle of Quebec seized upon this situation to revive their complaints against him.

Franklin's efforts failed even more shatteringly than those of his military predecessors. Canada had chosen and its choice was soon bolstered by the arrival of substantial British reinforcements. Arnold's rivals bungled the last chances of success, and on June 18, 1776, the American invasion of Canada ended in ignominy.

In that moment, so sad for his ambitions and for the American cause, Arnold seized one last moment of glory. In the retreat to New York he commanded the rear guard in a series of brave skirmishes, and then, with a gesture that somehow showed his despising for his fellow officers as much as his fearlessness in the face of the advancing enemy, he so arranged matters that he was the very last American to leave the Canadian shore.

Arnold had not lost confidence. He had been appreciated by Montgomery and, even more heartening, by Washington. The British knew him as "the most enterprising man among the rebels." He had proved himself as a leader and as a tactician. His courage had not faltered either in the hardships of the wilderness march or in the moments of catastrophe and physical pain. His only failing was one that he did not recognize his complete inability to tread the paths of diplomacy. Even when he was on the just side in a debate somehow he put himself in the wrong by arrogant behavior or intemperate comment; so that, for example, at the very moment when the disunited colonies were declaring themselves united and independent of Britain, Arnold once more came close to ending his services to the new nation before they had begun just because he treated with disdain a court set up to try one of his own enemies. The court martial for which he was responsible came close to arranging to court martial Benedict Arnold instead.

He survived that danger, though not without adding to the number of his influential enemies and to his own sense of grievance. Though accusations that he had enriched himself in the last months of the Canadian campaign still hung over him, Arnold, with his customary energy and skill, began a new task set for him by Washington: the creation and command of a fleet to match the British naval forces on Lake Champlain.

It can be argued that Arnold was even better as a naval commander than as a land-based general. He fought his ships with rare ability and won the entire respect of the highly experienced Royal Navy officers who met him in battle. His Lake Champlain campaign gave Washington time to prepare for the great British thrust that was intended to split New England from the middle and southern states. But, as in Canada so now on Lake Champlain, though Arnold could claim glory and no shame, he could not boast a victory. (And, through no fault of his the adventure might have ended in entire disaster had not his old adversary Carleton, like General Howe at about the same time, held back from the kill because he still hoped for reconciliation between Britain and America.)

Then, on February 19, 1777, Arnold suffered a blow to his prestige and pride more severe than any failure to gain a sensational victory, less comprehensible than the sniping attacks of enemies. Congress promoted five officers to the rank of major general. All had been beneath him in the order of seniority; the *unbreakable* convention that had been used to hold him from command in Canada after Montgomery's death was now broken five times over to thwart him of the promotion that was undeniably due to him also because he had shown capacities in the field which none of the five new major generals possessed or were ever to show.

What Arnold did not know when he received the news of this (to him) inexplicable and unforgivable rebuff was that Congress had not sought the advice of its commander-in-chief, but when, in a letter of such frankness as to be itself well-nigh insubordinate, Washington informed him of the facts and urged him not to do anything hasty, Arnold was already determined that he would go to Philadelphia to attempt to persuade Congress to change its mind and to clear his name of all the slights and calumnies to which he had been subjected since first he took up arms.

It was a risky course, more risky than he knew. Undoubtedly Congress had held back Arnold's promotion because of his cantankerous reputation. Undoubtedly his enemies were at work. Undoubtedly there were political considerations, such as the continuing need to satisfy the honor of all the contending states, which led Congress to sacrifice several other distinguished and worthy officers as well as Arnold. But all-unsuspecting Arnold was a victim of something far bigger than personal antagonism or interstate rivalry. He was caught in the struggle that had already begun in the United States and that will continue in all democracies until armies cease to be—the determination of the civil authority to limit the power of the military if need be by administering to the armed services an occasional severe snub, even when it is not deserved.

And now Arnold, a mere brigadier general, intended to question the rectitude of the civil power.

If Arnold did not appreciate the dangers (and he would not have hesitated had they been brought to his notice), British intelligence officers knew them all for they were equipped with long historical memories of similar confrontations between the military and Parliament. Eagerly the Arnold dossier was taken out, dusted off, read, and metaphorically marked "For Close Attention."

Arnold was action prone. Even when he intended a few days furlough in New Haven, he found himself engaged instead in a hot skirmish alongside the New Haven militia against a British army raiding into Connecticut. This time he came close to ending not only his career but also his life.

The action in Philadelphia was of a different kind, and nothing like so pleasing to Arnold. A pamphlet was on sale in the streets restating the charge that he had used his military authority to line his civilian pocket; and though Congress rejected the worst allegations of this scurrilous attack, it left in abeyance (and therefore as subject for continued suspicion) a full investigation of his accounts and refused out of hand his request that the matter of his rank be reconsidered.

On July 11, 1777, Arnold implemented the threat that he had mouthed to himself and to others almost since first he became a soldier. He delivered to Congress his letter of resignation, setting it in phrases which were undoubtedly heartfelt but which were also, even for the eighteenth century, remarkably pompous. "Honor is a sacrifice no man ought to make; as I received, so I wish to transmit it inviolate to posterity."

Happily for Arnold, Congress had just received another letter full of praise for him and calling upon the government to appoint him to the army commanded by General Schuyler, who was preparing to meet the renewed British threat to cut in two the United States by invading from Montreal and seizing the Hudson waterway. Arnold, Washington wrote, was "active, judicious and brave." He was also well acquainted with the country. The troops he would have to command were of indifferent quality, but Washington was persuaded that Arnold's leadership would inspire them.

Washington's advice was accepted. Arnold withdrew his resignation and agreed to serve as required, even though he knew that he might find himself in the field as a subordinate to some of those who had but recently leapfrogged over him in the order of seniority. Perhaps he still hoped that his acquiescence would change the mind of Congress. If so, he was again disappointed. A vote for restitution of his seniority was soundly defeated.

Up in the northern army, the generals were quarreling again. "They worry one another," wrote John Adams, "like mastiffs, scrambling for rank and pay like apes for nuts." At first Arnold was not involved directly. The struggle between generals Schuyler and Gates was for the overall command and thus far above Arnold's head. But he was in the field with Schuyler and therefore (probably mistakenly) thought by Gates to be a Schuyler's man. So eventually when Schuyler's military failures, Gates' political maneuverings, and the wisdom of Congress gave the command to Gates, Arnold was once more serving under a general who disliked him.

The consequence was as serious for the United States as it was for Arnold. Gates refused to accept Arnold's advice and consequently, at the Battle of Freeman's Farm (near Saratoga), missed one magnificent opportunity to destroy Burgoyne's advance. When Arnold complained that his own services and those of his division were not so much as mentioned in Gates' report to Congress, Gates replied that as Arnold had resigned his commission he had no military standing. Then, as if to make sure that he would get Arnold either way, he added that General Benjamin Lincoln was on his way to join the army and, once arrived, would take over from Arnold—a double insult because Lincoln was one of the five who had received accelerated promotion. "High words and gross language ensued." Finally, Gates told Arnold that his services were of little importance and that he could have a pass to go back to Philadelphia.

The pass did not come, which was just as well because Philadelphia had fallen to the British. A few senior officers made themselves almost as unpopular as Arnold by taking his side, while some of Arnold's juniors made the situation worse by complaining to Gates that Arnold had twice overruled the decision of a council of war. Gates continued to give scant courtesy to Arnold, omitting him even from those summoned to attend staff conferences.

Arnold was on the verge of hysteria when the situation was saved, not by Gates, not by Washington, not by Congress, not by Arnold himself, but by the errors of the British.

Burgoyne had not received the support he needed

from Canada, and though his forces had pressed deep into New York State his supplies were running short. Howe for his part had been slow to send a force out from New York. When finally it moved, under the command of General Clinton, it fought several successful battles, and the news of its impending arrival did not reach Burgoyne who decided upon a desperate attack at Bemis Heights on October 7, 1777.

Through the early part of the battle Arnold was virtually a prisoner within the American lines, held there by Gates's refusal to give him a command or even permission to fight as a volunteer. He watched, in a torment of frustration as, one after the other, American tactical commanders failed to take decisive action. Then, when it seemed that, despite their very heavy losses, the smaller British forces might somehow escape disaster, Arnold leaped into the battle. It was an act of undeniable insubordination but it was also madly heroic. This way lay death, a court martial, or great honor.

Arnold galloped into the battle shrieking encouragement and abuse at the American troops. His fury was directed at Gates rather than at the British, but it was the enemy who felt his sword, and even in his frenzy, he did not lose his tactical skill. This was his kind of action; he had never been, and was never to become, a strategist; but his personal courage and the quickness of decision which was his in the midst of battle made him one of the best of battlefield senior officers.

Arnold, the general who was denied by his own side the right to take part in the Battle of Bemis Heights, won the day, and that day was one of the most crucial of the whole war. But Arnold was wounded once more, in the same leg that was wounded at Quebec.

A week later, near Saratoga, Burgoyne's battered

army surrendered, Quebec was avenged, and for the first time the Americans had defeated a substantial regular force.

Perversely, the new nation which had refused Arnold his due glory when he had behaved more or less correctly, now chose to ignore his breach of proper military behavior. Gates won his share of praise but the hero of the hour was Benedict Arnold. Even Congress went with the tide of praise and, after some delay, restored his proper seniority. But Arnold had made yet one more immovable enemy: General Horatio Gates.

Arnold's often wounded pride was temporarily healed. His twice-wounded leg was slower to yield to treatment. In the last months of 1777 and the first of 1778 while Washington's army suffered in its winter quarters, Arnold suffered from pain and suffered more from inactivity, in Connecticut. When the French came into the war Arnold made no comment, though his personal hatred for Frenchmen and Catholics must have made this an alliance difficult to accept.

Even when he was summoned to join Washington at Valley Forge in May, it was clear that he could not hope for a field command. On May 28, he was appointed commander of Philadelphia, for the moment an honor without substance, for Philadelphia was still in British hands.

Two days later Arnold took the oath of allegiance required of all Continental officers:

> I Benedict Arnold Major General do acknowledge the United States of America to be Free, Independent and Sovereign States, and declare that the people thereof owe no allegiance or obedience to George the Third, King of Great Britain; and I renounce, refuse and abjure any allegiance or obedience to him; and I do swear that I

will to the utmost of my power, support, maintain and defend the said United States against the said King George the Third, his heirs and successors, and his or their abettors, assistants and adherents, and will serve the said United States in the office of Major General which I now hold, with fidelity, according to the best of my skill and understanding.

The oath seems irreproachable and unbreakable by any but a scoundrel. The fact that within months Arnold was feeling his way toward breaking it, and within three years had shattered it beyond belief, has through the centuries marked him as the worst of villains. Yet it is worth reiterating that oaths similar to that taken at Valley Forge have been the custom of all conspiracies and rebellions (including the Confederacy) and, therefore, though Arnold's subsequent actions are inexcusable, not too much need be made of the broken oath.

The convalescent Arnold came to his new command more speedily than even he had expected. Clinton's surprising evacuation of Philadelphia was completed on June 18, 1778. The next day Benedict Arnold issued his first proclamation as military commander of Philadelphia. Within weeks he was writing another proclamation, a love letter to a Philadelphia girl he had just met: Peggy Shippen. (The prying historian can know what Peggy never knew: the letter is close to being an exact repetition of another letter written by Arnold earlier that year to another young woman. Arnold's habitual extravagance did not extend to his literary endeavors.)

Almost from the moment of his arrival in Philadelphia Arnold had seemed set on continuing the convivialities that had marked the British occupation of the city. He saw no reason why an American general would cut a figure less elegant than that of his British predecessor. But, unlike Howe and Clinton, he lacked the social confidence to maintain his eminence without ostentation, and because he had few subordinates who were both able and willing to assist him in his extravagances, he, far more than Howe or Clinton, was the obvious center of all the dinners, dances, and entertainments at which he was either host or principal guest.

It was no way to make himself popular with the more rabid exponents of the revived American cause who chose to regard frivolity as in some odd way synonymous with Britishness and luxury as well-nigh treasonable. Nor did Arnold add to his reputation among the more severe Pennsylvanians by his seemingly careless choice of table companions and drinking partners. Many who had been notably hospitable to the British were allowed to entertain the American commander, and many who had not been politically or socially uncomfortable during the British occupation were on Arnold's guest list. He could have answered any criticism of his easygoing sociability with the retort that he chose to spend his private hours with the liveliest people of Philadelphia. A latter-day advocate can urge for him that, at least theoretically, his political acumen was sharper than that of his detractors and that his affability to those whose loyalties were uncertain or undecided followed the sensible British precedent. But in Philadelphia the time for persuasion was past; the city had changed hands too recently and was gripped by an hysteria against collaborators and Loyalists such as was not common during the Revolution.

Worse still for Arnold's present popularity and future success, his enemies were snapping at his heels, and he was forever adding to the size of the pack. His motives were pathetically easy to misconstrue. If he chose to be easygoing with those who had been easygoing with the British he could be accused of aiding and abetting the enemy. When he attempted to enforce discipline he could be held to treat honest and upright Americans with severity which he would not use against Loyalists. And those who were bent on his destruction were quick to link his apparent extravagance with the old smear that he used his public position to fill his private coffers—an assertion that the prodigality of his spending did nothing to deny.

Already before Arnold proposed to Peggy Shippen he was in greater danger from his fellow Americans than from the British. There were many in the Council of Pennsylvania who were talking openly of bringing to trial the American general commanding in Philadelphia.

Arnold's unenviable situation almost caused him to lose Peggy Shippen. Her father prevaricated, offering excuse after excuse for deferring his consent—the age-difference between the two, Arnold's wounds, his three children, the uncertainty of the times—but never mentioning the undoubted fact that Shippen's own conscience was much sensitized by the knowledge that all Pennsylvania knew that he and his family had been cordial to British officers. Peggy too, was not quick to make up her mind, according to the legend (which unlike so many legends in the Arnold-André story cannot be supported by any evidence), because she was still pining for John André. But finally, in the spring of 1779, Peggy and her father agreed that she would become the second Mrs. Benedict Arnold.

Arnold was as excited as a boy, and it was as a boy and not as a mature general that he set about making

Mount Pleasant, the house Arnold bought but never occupied. *Courtesy of The Historical Society of Pennsylvania.*

Penn Cottage where Arnold lived with his young bride while military governor of Philadelphia. *Courtesy of The Historical Society of Pennsylvania.*

preparations for the future which would confirm his enemies in their worst suspicions and confound even his few defenders. The Shippens were by Philadelphia standards aristocrats. Arnold must demonstrate his right to marry into the family by buying for Peggy one of Philadelphia's most undeniably aristocratic houses. Mount Pleasant stood in a park of one hundred acres and was, according to John Adams, "the most elegant seat in Pennsylvania."

The Arnolds never lived in Mount Pleasant. On April 8, 1779, the two were married. "Arnold during the ceremony was supported by a soldier, and when seated his disabled limb was propped upon a stool." After the ceremony the couple moved into the house allotted to the commander of Philadelphia, the house of William Penn.

4. André and Arnold

To HIS FIRST wife Arnold had shown qualities of tenderness such as he had previously demonstrated to no other human being except his mother. His love for the second Peggy was certainly no less profound, but it was for him more exciting. Peggy adored him, but not in any meek or placid way, for in marriage the flirtatious girl soon became a vigorous and sensual woman. Such a relationship, which flared occasionally into violence, suited well his tempestuous nature, but Arnold was older now—and very much older than his wife. He was also worn down by wounds, frustrations, and a sense of persecution; and as the need for flaunting his second successful marriage before his countrymen became obsessive, so too did his need to demonstrate to Peggy his superiority over all others that she might have chosen as provider, patriot, and soldier. Peggy, for her part, did nothing to temper his ostentation and much to strengthen his sense of grievance against those who persecuted him. She had skeletons in her own closet. Even though in retrospect it may seem harsh to condemn an eighteen-year-old girl for dancing with a British officer, Philadelphia at that time was ready to regard such behavior as treasonable. And Peggy, in this like her husband, was not given to penitence. Instead she encouraged in her husband leniency toward her former friends, Tories and suspected Tories, and thus bolstered in the military governor of Philadelphia an inclination toward a policy which he could justify as also good military sense. She may have gone further; perhaps all the way toward inciting him to treasonable thoughts, and certainly as far as listening, without protest, to his growing distaste for the American cause.

Ostentation and appeasement added to the number of those who were set upon ruining Arnold, and both ostentation and appeasement gave to his enemies their opportunity.

The heart and head of this enmity was the Council of Pennsylvania, and early in 1779 the Council decided that its time had come. A list of charges against Arnold was drawn up and forwarded to Congress. They were, most of them, half-truths based either upon Arnold's obvious proclivity for making money in a manner that can be described (according to the sympathies of the commentator) either as careless or vicious, upon his undeniable arrogance, and upon his refusal to go all the way toward persecuting the Tories.

A committee of Congress cleared Arnold of a few of the charges against him, advised that others could only be judged by recourse to the civil courts, and that some, being entirely a matter of martial law, must be referred to General Washington.

The committee had done its best to be fair and indeed had done more than its best for Arnold, and there were congressmen who were well aware, as one of them put it, that the Council of Pennsylvania was behaving in a "waspish, peevish and childish" fashion. But issues of greater consequence were at stake than the reputation of one American general. The frail threads which bound the thirteen ex-colonies together had to be preserved even if they could not as yet be strengthened. Congress as a whole was unwilling to risk a collision with the powerful and implacable patriots of Pennsylvania.

Arnold recognized the political necessity.

> If Congress have been induced to take this action for the public good [he wrote to Washington on 14 April 1779] and to avoid a breach with this state, however hard my case may be and however I am injured as an individual, I will suffer with pleasure until a court-martial can have the opportunity of doing me justice by acquitting me . . . .

But his forbearance was only intellect-deep. His much-battered pride was ready for some balm that not even acquittal could provide, and his conscience must have made him aware that on some of the charges—especially those relating to misappropriation of funds—acquittal was improbable. Meanwhile, his enemies launched against him a new series of attacks in the press that took the record of his misdoings back almost to the beginning of his military career and demanded of Washington successive postponements of court-martial in order that they might gather together more evidence.

On May 5, 1779, Arnold abandoned all pretenses of patience and wrote to Washington:

> If your Excellency thinks me criminal, for heaven's sake let me be immediately tried and, if found guilty, executed . . . . Let me beg you, Sir to consider that a set of artful, unprincipled men in office may misrepresent the most innocent actions and, by raising the public clamour against your Excellency, place you in the same situation I am in. Having made every sacrifice of fortune and blood, and become a cripple in the service of my country, I little expected to meet the ungrateful returns I

have received from my countrymen, but as Congress
have stamped ingratitude as a current coin, I must take
it.

Arnold had suffered, though not in his pocket. And it is a
question whether this letter was in truth what it appears
to be: a plea for quick justice sent from one soldier to
another, or whether it was instead a preface to the
self-justification for what was already in his mind, sent by
Arnold to one of the very few among his superiors for
whom he had entire respect. And when, nine days later,
in a seemingly calmer mood Arnold wrote again to
Washington stating his wish to return to active duty "as
soon as my wounds will permit," was this in reality a
reiteration of innocence and loyalty or was he hedging
his bets? It could be that he was saying, if only to himself,
that, given the right answer by Washington, then he
would be prepared to fight on for the American cause,
and, if the right answer was not forthcoming, then. . . .
    What is certain is that between the two letters, the
Arnold file was made active in Major André's intelligence
office in New York and at Arnold's instigation. On May
10, 1779, his emissary, Joseph Stansbury, called upon
André to test the temperature of British water.
    Although British intelligence had long considered
Arnold as a potential turncoat, the abruptness of this
approach took even the bland and experienced André by
surprise, the more so as he was at the time unwell and, as
he put it on the same day to his superior officer, Sir
Henry Clinton, in no condition to resist "the kind of
Confusion such Sudden proposals created when one
must deliberate and determine at once." But *at once* it
must be lest Stansbury be missed from his familiar
haunts in Philadelphia or expose himself to too many

risks of being identified by an American agent in New York. So André shook from himself the torpor of an invalid and within very short time had constructed not merely a brief for Arnold that offered to him a wide selection of possible treacherous acts but also a system of communication between the putative traitor and British intelligence which included messengers, secret inks, cyphers, and code books. Significantly André accepted for Arnold the pseudonym Monck, as if to honor by association his actions with those of the Cromwellian turned Royalist. Not then, nor ever until almost the tragic end of the story, was there revealed even in the communication between André and his superiors, so much as a flicker of repugnance for Arnold's behavior such as comes frequently from soldiers who must use tools they cannot respect. Arnold would have to be rewarded, this André made clear, but so had General Monck been repaid with money and honors for the risks that he had taken in 1660 when returning Englishmen to their proper loyalty to the Crown.

The cloak-and-dagger scenario prepared by André on that Monday in May contained a strong hint that he had been in touch previously with Peggy Arnold about matters more vital than fashion, and a clear indication that at very least Peggy was party to her husband's overtures. As one possible line of communication André suggested an innocent-seeming correspondence between himself and Peggy Chew, his partner at the famous Mischianza (which he now called "a nonsense"). Peggy Chew was to remain ignorant of the true purpose of the letter, but she was to be persuaded to show to Peggy Arnold what he had written and to route her replies by way of Mrs. Arnold who would add the cypher indication and the messages in secret ink.

By one means or another, communication between Arnold and André developed. It did not prosper consistently. Several letters were lost. On one occasion, when subjected to heat, the secret ink ran before the message could be read. Twice one of the conspirators used the wrong code book. What is perhaps surprising to a generation reared on sophisticated spy stories is the navieté of the attempts at secrecy. Arnold signed himself as G.A. (General Arnold). Sir Henry Clinton is but thinly disguised as S.H.C., and one letter opens with a reference in clear to the book that is to be used as a key for the rest of the coded message. Far less surprising is the fact that Arnold soon discovered that the British expected more of a Monck than mere protestations of changed loyalty. They wanted information, action, tangible proof that he could deliver and that what he had to deliver was worth the assurances and rewards that he sought.

Arnold did his best to demonstrate the genuine nature of his intentions but most of the information that he had to offer was based on little more than general military and political gossip which was as familiar to André as to Arnold. And although Arnold boasted that he had sources of intelligence even in Congress, he knew—or if he did not know, was soon forced to accept André's polite hints as brutal statements—that he had, in truth, not much to give to the British. The military governor of Philadelphia was a base-area commander of no great significance who received very little vital information and who was certainly in no position to achieve what André wanted from him: "concerting the means of a blow of importance." In both his secret and his public papers for the year 1779 (read with some knowledge of the psychology of treachery), the facts stand out clear from the pages: Arnold was now insuring against every possibility. If the American court-martial found in his favor there were still two opportunities open to him.

If a new command suited his vanity he could collect the back pay that was due to him and serve on to glory in the Continental Army. But, even then, it would be useful to be able to present to Washington some proof of his worth that would transcend even his distinguished record of service and his declared innocence. With the excuse that only with such information available to him could he choose wisely his moment of desertion, Arnold pressed André for advance news of British intentions.

Or, if he so desired, even after the court-martial had found for him, still he could go over to the British if the terms were right.

But, if the Americans continued to dishonor him, then he must act according to his not-unjustified assumption that Washington was on his side and would not see him utterly disgraced. And by pretending that he wished to redeem himself in action, he must drag from the commander-in-chief a posting that would make his treason a saleable commodity.

Whichever side was to be honored by honoring him, whether he was to betray his fellow Americans or serve as a double agent against the British, Arnold must have a good command.

But, for the moment, the British no less than the Americans seemed disinclined to give Arnold what he regarded as his just deserts. André would give nothing for nothing. His enthusiasm for the plot diminished and, although he kept open his line of communication with Arnold by way of courteous letters to Peggy, his hope that he would lure a prominent American leader into an act of treachery shifted somewhat toward Arnold's old rival, Ethan Allen.

Arnold's pride was bruised by this rebuff and he wrote letters full of rebukes to Clinton for those who would not trust him. But, meanwhile, he had to reshape the defense of his maligned integrity so that he could face the court-martial convened in Washington's camp on June 1.

In matters of business, in his private life, and as a tactician, Arnold was never content to wait upon events. So now, even in the presence of the commander-in-chief, Arnold insisted on laying about him, impugning those who had brought him to the edge of disgrace as villains and rogues, and reiterating the proud tale of his achievements. Washington, who had done his best to provide a court that would be inclined to favor an active-service soldier with a brave record, nonetheless resented this preempting of the court's procedures and (though without much success) tried to bring home to Arnold some realization that he was being both foolish and impertinent.

However, it was through no fault of Washington (nor indeed of Arnold) that the court had to be adjourned before it had heard any evidence. The accidental intervention of Sir Henry Clinton, who at this very moment launched an expedition up the Hudson, made it imperative for Washington to return all the senior officers to their units who were to have judged Arnold. And it was not until the Christmas week of 1779 that a new court could be brought together at Morristown.

The English-born, Judge Advocate General John Lawrence, properly ignored all those original charges against Arnold which had been rejected by Congress.

But Arnold would have none of such legal precision. In speeches of inordinate length, his voice shaking with indignation, he refuted every charge made by the Council of Pennsylvania and repeated for the court's benefit his heroic military autobiography. Nor was this all. As so often when under attack he behaved as if he were the accuser rather than the accused. A ruse, perhaps, or a diversion, but such was Arnold's character and his vast capacity for self-justification that it seems more likely that when he rounded upon his enemies his conscience knew no rub and he saw no reason in his current behavior to make him hesitate before naming others as traitors to the American cause.

The court was not aware that the man who stood before them like an indignant St. Peter naming others as Judas, was himself haggling for more pieces of silver. Instead, with entire propriety because they had not been asked to judge him on many of the charges against which he protested with such vigor, the officers of the court gave no response, (either favorable or unfavorable) to much of his defense and passed no comment on his counter charges. But even on the limited case presented by the judge advocate general, the court-martial handed down a decision that was notably lenient. On three of their five charges Arnold was acquitted, on a fourth it was found that although Arnold had not committed any offense under military law he had acted imprudently. Only on one comparatively minor charge was he judged as guilty. He was sentenced "to receive a reprimand from his Excellency the commander-in-chief."

Washington tempered the reprimand with praise for Arnold's previous service, but Arnold was in no mood to be mollified. He erased from his mind and from his letters all reference to the one count on which he had been found guilty, took Washington's praise at its face value, but the General's reprimand as yet another proof of the helplessness of soldiers against the villainy of politicians. He proceeded to argue that if he were innocent he could not have behaved imprudently and that if he were brave no reprimand could be meant.

The doubleness of his nature and his advanced sense of grievance made such illogicality inevitable. Here, once more was persecution, but here also was justification and a chance to wipe the slate clean so that he could move forward to promotion—whether in the British or the American army he was even now not certain.

There followed more activity on Arnold's part that hindsight can interpret in a variety of ways. All Continental officers needed money; the debased American currency left most of them far short of their requirements. But Arnold, with an expensive wife and expensive tastes, needed money more than almost any of his contemporaries. Congress was still insisting that Arnold owed to the government money that had not been repaid after the Canadian campaign four years earlier. Arnold had always insisted that the debt was on the other side and that he was due a considerable sum. Now (and with some justice) he asked for a decision. At the same time he suggested to Washington and to the Navy board that he be given a naval command; and if he did not mention this part of his ambition to his superiors, it must have been in his mind that in the eighteenth century successful naval operations brought to their commanders not only glory but also prize money. Almost certainly he also sought a loan from the French ambassador.

All this could be, and at the time could be seen to

be, no more reprehensible than a desire on Arnold's part to set in order his financial affairs. And even now it could be comfortably explained by the fact that Peggy was pregnant and he was expecting to return to active duty. Such a combination of circumstances has persuaded many a man to a consideration of his balance sheet.

But there could be more sinister explanations. If Arnold was going to risk all on a change of allegiance, then now was the moment to get all he could from the Americans and a little more from the French (who would never be able to reclaim money lent to an enemy officer). Even he could add some shine to his reputation with the British if he could go to them after having reduced by however insignificant a sum the exchequers of both their enemies. As for the naval command, André had suggested that he look to be posted to the leadership of a cavalry division because a cavalry general has excellent opportunities for surrendering his force to the enemy. How much better would be the chances open to a commander of a naval squadron.

Arnold achieved none of his immediate aims, not the naval command, not the French loan, or indeed a settlement of his financial dispute with Congress; and once more the rebuffs added to his sense of being always persecuted. In particular, the pernicious dilatoriness of Congress added also to his feeling that treason against a political organization which treated its servants with such disdain could not be considered treason at all, that he who helps to overthrow a corrupt, inefficient, and ungrateful government is not a traitor.

Arnold's resentment for the dilatoriness of Congress and the malice of the Council of Pennsylvania aroused some sympathetic response in his commander-in-chief. During his long military career Washington had suffered frequently from the insensitivity shown by politicians and administrators to the practical problems of commanders in the field, but never before had he had such good reason for despair at civilian ineptitude or distaste for civil mishandling of military affairs as now in the spring of 1780. The British had not succeeded in beating his army, but what the enemy had failed to achieve even in the miserable months at Valley Forge might soon be brought about by the indecisiveness of Congress and the bitter jealousies between the state governments. Officers were destitute, the army short of rations, clothing, and equipment. Washington himself described the situation as "melancholy"; others went further and pointed out that there was in all ranks "a spirit of discontent."

This widespread malaise bemused Washington. His subordinate's imprudence and occasional impertinence could be seen at worst as a symptom of the discontent which was gripping so many under his command. And he was even more inclined to regard it as evidence of Arnold's uncontrollable zeal and impatience to be active against all enemies, be they British or American, and therefore, in a sense, something to be admired. Further, at a time when the morale of all ranks was so shaken, Washington could not afford to be without the services of one who, whatever his faults, was without doubt a born leader and notably popular with those very elements whose zeal for the war was now most in question: the men of the state militias.

On the other hand, the disaffection that was rife in the Continental Army acted upon Arnold as ultimate persuader. He was at last convinced that there was no military future for the Revolution and that a decisive act on his part would clarify the minds of many of his countrymen.

But still he had not found a role which would allow him to indulge in action sufficiently important to serve as a lead for others or to satisfy André's demand that his change of coat be dramatic and of itself influential upon the strategic balance between the two armies and thus of such consequence as to bring to Arnold from the British the rank and wealth denied to him by the Americans because of personal animosity and economic and military breakdown.

Once more he surveyed the opportunities and this time settled his ambitions upon the fortress at West Point and the considerable military area under its command. This key position, if he could secure it for himself and then surrender it to the British, would be the "service of some importance" for which André was haggling. With considerable cunning, Arnold set about the task of manipulating Washington's goodwill, the support of influential Americans (who were entirely ignorant of his true motives), and the eagerness of the British.

The road to treason was paved with good luck. Because he could not ask openly for West Point he needed time for duping the American command into believing that the choice was its own. To this end, and although he could not see it at the time, even the temporary absence from New York of André, who was off campaigning in South Carolina with Clinton, worked to Arnold's advantage. For André would have treated with some impatience new overtures from a potential traitor unless Arnold had been able to offer something more substantial than the same worn-out vagueness that had caused André to lose interest the year before.

As events developed, by midsummer 1780 when André returned to New York, Arnold was able to offer him not only a certain amount of conventional intelligence information but, far more important,

advance notice of his posting to West Point. His price
was up:

> If I point out a plan of cooperation by which Sir Henry
> shall   possess   himself   of   West   Point,   the
> garrison &c. &c. &c. twenty thousand pounds sterling
> I think will be a cheap purchase . . . .

But it was worth it to André, who did not know that now,
as so often, Arnold was offering more than he could
deliver. By careful manipulation of his innocent allies
and his commander-in-chief, Arnold had persuaded
Washington that though Arnold deserved a command
more important than Philadelphia, his wounds made it
unlikely that he could serve in the field. With a shrewd
and irrefutable report on the inadequacies of the West
Point defenses he had brought to Washington's mind the
probability that Arnold was right for West Point and
West Point right for Arnold. But though Arnold was
relieved from his command in Philadelphia, Washington's decision on his future was not settled when Arnold
insinuated to André that West Point was his to
surrender.

Indeed, at the beginning of August, Washington
offered to Arnold the command of the left flank of the
American army in the field. The offer came as a shock to
Arnold, for this would be a fulfilment of military
ambitions and would redress for all time the slights and
frustrations that he had suffered. But by now Arnold was
along the road to treason and was certain of American
weakness. He hurried to Washington's headquarters
and, insisting upon his physical infirmities, begged
Washington to appoint him to West Point.

The order was given, and on August 5, 1780, Arnold

set up house at the home of Colonel Beverly Robinson, two miles southeast of West Point on the opposite bank of the Hudson.

Immediately he sent one of his aides to bring Peggy from Philadelphia. As a general he had every right to have his wife at his side; as a lover he wanted her to be with him; as a traitor he no longer needed her to serve as his Philadelphia intermediary with the British; and, after his treason had been consummated, it would have been folly to leave Peggy as a hostage among the Americans.

It was easier to end his impatience with separation from his wife than it was to persuade the British to accept that he meant to live by his promises. The sums of money that he demanded, the indemnities that he required, and the rank in the British army that he insisted must be his were not too much to pay for West Point and for the damage to American strategic positioning and morale that would follow upon Arnold's surrender. However, Arnold wanted considerable payment in advance, and André, as dispassionate in his role of intelligence adviser as he was passionate in his wish to end the American rebellion, still lacked proof that Arnold either would or could deliver all that he had promised.

Arnold was in a quandary. Any premature attempt to prove himself to the British—for example, by weakening the fortifications or the tactical dispositions around West Point—might lose him all. There would be no rewards from Britain if his plans miscarried and from the Americans only dishonor and, perhaps, death. Yet André would offer little more than the price of a new wardrobe for Peggy until he was sure of his man.

For a few weeks, at the end of August and early in September 1780 Arnold fenced not only with André but also at the same time with his American colleagues as well.

In geographical terms they were closer together than ever before, separated only by the undecided territory between the American and British forces along the Hudson. But an important link in their chain of communications had been broken by Peggy's move to West Point. Both men, but Arnold even more urgently than André, sought some new and reliable messengers. Arnold saw a threefold opportunity. If he could discover the names of agents who brought to the Americans information from New York, then he might discover one who would serve his purpose instead of the American cause. Even if none would fit this role, a list of enemy spies must be a present that would convince the British that Arnold was a genuine turncoat. And, most important, if Arnold could identify the spies he could also guard his own secrets from them and thus reduce the chance of premature discovery of his plot.

He put the question directly to his predecessor at West Point and to Lafayette. Nothing in this act was notably dangerous. A general officer commanding in an area so close to the enemy has every right to be aware of intelligence operations. And though Arnold's request for information was firmly, if politely rejected, no-one on the American side suspected his motives, although, as came out later, at least one American agent in New York had somehow stumbled on the fact that a senior Continental officer was preparing to sell out to the British and had reported his discovery to Washington's headquarters.

Arnold had to look elsewhere for a new intermediary and hit upon Joshua Hett Smith, the brother of the Loyalist chief justice of New York, but himself, at least ostensibly, a good American patriot.

André, however, was not content with any intermediary. He needed to assess Arnold's character. If then he were satisfied that Arnold would fulfill his promise, still it would be wise for the two to meet so that André could instruct Arnold in the detail, the timing, and the manner of his final acts of betrayal. He suggested that they arrange a rendezvous at some place in the no-man's land between the two armies. Arnold, who also wanted a meeting to seal the bargain, countered with the proposal that André come to him under a flag of truce, and, even before an answer was received prepared the way for such a visit by informing the commanders of his outposts that he was expecting on private and innocent business a New York merchant named John Anderson. (Still the initials J.A. For a time during the negotiations the British had reduced Arnold from "Monck" to "Moore"; Arnold preferred G.A., for General Arnold, but filled out the initials by calling himself "Gustavus Adolphus," thus demonstrating not only his vainglory but also his despising of the Catholic French. For among the soldier heroes of Prostestantism, there was only one rival to the king of Sweden as the greatest of them all, and Arnold could hardly call himself Oliver Cromwell!)

The British looked carefully at Arnold's proposal and found it sensible and reasonable. Arnold was a well-known figure and easily identifiable. The chances were high that his presence, at some place where he had no good reason to be and in strange company, would be reported to Washington, and even though he might be able to fabricate some explanation, the suspicion that would follow must undermine his potential usefulness to the British. It was not unreasonable that Arnold would not play his part unless cued by an officer armed with authority. André had handled most of the preliminary negotiations and he was in effect Clinton's voice. Nor did the risks seem great. Although André was not unknown his appearance was not, like Arnold's, common knowledge, and even were he recognized by an American informer, many excuses could be invented for his presence. It was by no means unusual for officers of the opposing armies to meet for administrative discussions, and there was no reason to suppose that the Americans would disregard a flag of truce that had been accepted by their senior officer on the spot. There were, at all events, additional safeguards that could be imposed. For example, the rendezvous could be so arranged as to be clearly within the area of Arnold's command but at some place where American troops were thin in the ground, from whence it would be comparatively simple for André to escape to the British lines.

What remained to be decided was whether it was worth continuing the plot with Arnold, and, on consideration, all doubts faded.

Clinton needed a substantial victory. His forces were overstretched. The British public, no less than the American, was divided about the rights and wrongs of the American war, and Parliament was showing more than its habitual reluctance to spend men and money on suppressing a rebellion in distant colonies. But Clinton, as he considered the situation of the enemy, was reaffirmed in his conviction that the moment had come when he must risk the venture. The thought that Benedict Arnold, druggist and traitor of New Haven, was asking to be appointed a brigadier-general in His Majesty's Service might nauseate Clinton, and his humor was not improved by the £20,000 pill that Arnold was asking him to swallow. But Clinton could not allow his distaste for Arnold to override his military shrewdness. The probability that he could control the Hudson and thus divide the Americans in New England from their compatriots to the South was too rich for scruple.

Rumor added to his eagerness. The story had come to him (from Arnold) that, if he acted quickly, there might be a chance of capturing "Mr. Washington."

His appreciation of the situation was exact, and he knew that he must send André to make the final arrangements that would turn this appreciation into an accomplishment. But still there were doubts nagging at the commander.

General Sir Henry Clinton was not the kind of man to believe in premonitions. Yet, at the time when he prepared André for his mission, he was undoubtedly troubled and showed his perturbation by frequent repetition of his instructions. He had come to respect his adjutant-general. Together they had considered both the implications of Arnold's offer and the detail of André's journey to West Point; and Clinton could find no flaws in the mutually rehearsed arguments that had persuaded them to accept the need for a rendezvous nor yet any sinister gaps in the planning for that rendezvous. But Clinton had also learned affection for André, and as he looked upon André with an almost paternal eye, he came close to realizing that certain dangers were after all inherent in the situation and that these dangers sprang primarily from the character of John André.

André knew no fear except the fear of boredom. As a staff officer he could be properly cautious, but even in that capacity he had revealed sometimes the same love of the dramatic that was so obvious in his social behavior. Clinton realized that, once André was freed from the inhibitions that came with day-to-day contact with superiors and subordinates his histrionic nature might well take over, that once the solo performance was started André would be inclined to act it out to the final curtain.

Clinton recognized, too, that André's unshakable

loyalty to the Crown might reduce his capacity for judging Arnold. Unlike his more cynical general, who knew that Arnold was a traitor, despised him for it, and mistrusted all his actions, André was close to believing that Arnold was indeed the American General Monck.

Consequently Clinton's instructions were both explicit and reiterated. Admiral Rodney's squadron had arrived off New York and relieved Clinton of some of his anxieties about the French fleet hovering threateningly in the Atlantic. He could release a force for the dash to West Point, but André must impress upon Arnold that there could be no delays. As for the meeting between the two, there was a British sloop in the Hudson, H.M.S. *Vulture* (Captain Andrew Sutherland commanding) stationed not 15 miles from Arnold's headquarters in the wide section of the river known as Haverstraw Bay. This ship, a familiar sight to the Americans manning the forts at King's Ferry and Verplanck Point, could serve as André's base. But first *Vulture* must be withdrawn farther from West Point, nearer to the British lines, and it must be there, somewhere in the area of Dobbs Ferry, that André and Arnold should meet. André was to go openly as a British officer. Under no circumstances was he to adopt a disguise. Arnold must come to him and nothing should be allowed to lure André within the American lines.

In other circumstances André, a man with an imagination far more sensitive than Clinton's, might well have experienced those trembling foretastes of disaster that are not uncommon among soldiers just before action, but at this moment his mind's eye was looking far beyond his meeting with Arnold—to the promotion that would be his after West Point had fallen and to the knighthood that would be his reward if Arnold's defection brought about the end of what was, for André, a senseless rebellion. At all events, there was by André's reckoning nothing especially hazardous in his mission.

The messages preparatory to their meeting, couched as usual in commercial terms, went from André to Arnold on September 7, and four days later André was at Dobbs Ferry. There was some inconsequential skirmishing along the river that day and Arnold thought it best to forego the rendezvous. André went back to New York and held his impatience in check by polishing the third part of his ballad *The Cow-Chase*, a by no means good-natured satire about General Anthony Wayne.

Benedict and Peggy Arnold had no diversion to relax their tension. Indeed with Washington, Lafayette, and several other senior Continental officers in and out of their home and headquarters each day, the chances of discovery seemed inevitable. Arnold explained himself to the British and urged that "John Anderson" come once more to Dobbs Ferry.

So, at sunrise on September 20, 1780, John André boarded his barge. The briskness of a fall morning must have matched his eagerness to be on to his meeting with Arnold, to be on to the moment of decision, to be on to promotion and glory.

The disruption of all the plans that had been seemingly so carefully laid was caused in part by a series of accidents. Clandestine arrangements are by their very nature never so thorough as to allow for accident. Blame for the eventual tragedy can be laid to many men, to Washington, the unbending patriot, and to Arnold, the turncoat. But, though his rectitude is beyond question, some responsibility for the consequences must be borne by André, the unfortunate victim. Clinton's doubts were proved valid; André was just too eager.

André arrived at Dobbs Ferry in midafternoon and

should have waited for *Vulture*. Instead, as the tide was with him, he pressed on to Haverstraw Bay and, once aboard *Vulture*, found himself in an atmosphere of tension that was by no means typical of a well-ordered man-of-war whose officers and crew were hardened to service on an exposed station. That morning a boat, sent by the captain to investigate a white flag, had been fired upon by the very American outpost which had hoisted the signal. Such a flagrant breach of military courtesy would have infuriated Sutherland at any time, but now, having some inkling of the business upon which André was engaged, he read sinister significance into the incident. The Americans, he felt, were baiting a trap; whether for *Vulture*, for his passenger, the Loyalist Colonel Beverly Robinson, or for André, he did not know. Robinson, whose overt business with his enemies was entirely legitimate, shared Sutherland's suspicions. He, more than the naval captain, was party to the reasons for André's presence and he knew that his negotiations about his confiscated property were being used as part of the cover story for the proposed meeting between Arnold and André. Although he could not comprehend the motives for the morning occurrence, he was convinced that somehow it was connected with André's mission. And, when he heard what had happened, even André had it in mind that Arnold had staged the affair as some kind of a message to him—perhaps a warning.

There is no evidence that the firing on the white flag was anything but an act of indiscipline, and it is clear that Arnold had no part in it. In those crucial hours Arnold's manner toward the senior colleagues who visited him was at one moment blatantly boisterous and at the next remarkably reticent; it was an indication, as some of those colleagues reported, after the conspiracy had collapsed, that his conscience was at work persuading him to hold back from the terrible thing that he had planned to do. Other colleagues interpreted it as evidence of the typical weakness of the guilty minded—the inability to act naturally. Arnold was torn between a bursting desire to talk to somebody about anything and a conscious attempt to say nothing about anything to anybody lest he let slip some clue to his intentions.

Out on *Vulture* André assessed the situation. For him it was no longer a matter of looking into the mind of a man he had never met. He knew, as certainly as if he had seen Arnold being piped aboard, that it was no longer within Arnold's power to return to his American loyalties. Whatever last-minute fears, whatever flutterings of conscience Arnold might experience, he must come over to the British or be ruined by the British. Fail them now, and all that André had to do to ensure Arnold's downfall was to see to it that a copy of the Arnold dossier fell into American hands. Arnold was surrounded with American enemies who would believe any calumny about him and would certainly give him no opportunity to argue his way out of the most damning evidence that had ever been presented against an American general. And André knew that Arnold must appreciate the situation and must know that, if he failed them, the British would show to him no mercy.

Thus, André, although accepting the white-flag incident might have been arranged by Arnold, could not believe that it implied double-dealing. Instead, drawing a correct conclusion from evidence that was partially false, he coupled this irrelevant incident with his knowledge that Washington and Lafayette were in the vicinity and assumed that Arnold was having difficulties in escaping from their inquisitive eyes.

This assessment served as a brake upon André's

impatience as he waited for Arnold throughout the whole of that first night, the night on which Arnold had hinted that he might come out to *Vulture*. And even when dawn arrived but not Arnold, André held to his conviction that Arnold's visit had been prevented by force of circumstances and not by any new or fundamental decision.

Even so, Arnold's failure to make the rendezvous placed André in a dilemma. His orders were clear. If Arnold appeared to be holding back from fulfulling such minor obligations as were prefatory to his major obligation to defect, then André was to return immediately to New York. He knew too that although Sutherland was not party to all the details of the conspiracy, he was sufficiently informed to question the advisability of André staking all by remaining too long away from headquarters. Even had no substantial risk to the secret service plans been involved, still Sutherland would have seen it as his military duty to prevent the adjutant-general from staying in a forward position, close to the enemy's guns. And Sutherland outranked André. But rather than test the niceties of rank, André pretended a recurrence of his recent illness and asked to be allowed to stay aboard *Vulture* until he was fit for the return journey. He prepared a despatch for Clinton in which he admitted to the subterfuge. A seemingly impertinent gesture but not too risky for, by the time that the confession could reach Clinton, either the fate of West Point would be sealed and André would be a hero to whom all would be forgiven, or else the whole conspiracy would have collapsed and André himself would be back in New York to temper the abruptness of his written explanation with his habitual charm and lucidity.

As he waited through the hours of September 21, it was not danger from the Americans or Clinton's disapproval that he considered but the grim possibility that all his efforts with Arnold might come to nothing. He fretted so much that his feigned sickness came close to being a reality, and when in the early hours of September 22 a boat with muffled oars approached *Vulture*, he was too exhausted to leave his cabin to investigate. The news brought by the officer of the watch was not what he had hoped to hear. Arnold was still ashore at Smith's house in Belmont. Smith was aboard *Vulture* and he had with him a safe conduct for John Anderson from General Arnold and, also signed by Arnold, a letter to Colonel Robinson purporting to be no more than an agreement to meet with him at "a place of Safety" to discuss the sequestered property.

André knew that he must make the best of the situation as it was, and now neither Sutherland nor Robinson could deflect André's eagerness to go ashore to meet the man he had played for so long. Belmont was close to Haverstraw, only a few miles from where *Vulture* lay and outside the West Point defensive positions. There was no doubt that after the meeting André could return the way he had gone. Even better, by combining the two messages, by pretending to serve as Robinson's agent and then, if necessary, by trumping the Arnold-Robinson letter with the safe conduct made out in his own assumed name, André was so confident that, at the time, he did not notice that Smith's boat was not flying a flag of truce, and even the much more timorous Smith, who had been specifically assured by Arnold on this very point, was sufficiently complacent about the security of his mission to allow the omission to go unrectified.

Smith and André were rowed ashore; André was in his regimentals, having refused Sutherland's last-minute offer of a civilian greatcoat.

In the fir woods at Long Clove, a short distance from Haverstraw, seven miles from Stony Point and some way below the American lines, John André at last met Benedict Arnold. Two brave and efficient soldiers, both driven by ambition, had come together. Behind them lay months of planning for this moment, between them, perhaps, the shadow of Peggy Arnold, before them the knowledge that together they could achieve the salvation of an empire, the destruction of a cause, glory and promotion for André, gold and honors for Arnold.

But a wood by the Hudson is no place, and the middle of a late September night no time, for the care that must go into the successful planning of major acts of treason. Arnold had never intended that this would be anything more than a preliminary rendezvous. He had with him none of the papers that André had to see, but he had brought a spare horse so that André could ride with him back to Smith's house.

For André, having come this far, there was no alternative but to go the whole way. He mounted and, leaving behind them Joshua Smith, Arnold's groom, and on the river's edge the boatmen (who had already refused to wait to take André back to *Vulture*), the two officers rode off toward Haverstraw.

As they approached the village they were challenged by American sentries posted there by Arnold, presumably to guard himself against discovery by his colleagues, but also, perhaps, to provide for himself a cover story. If, despite all his precautions, some prying American found Arnold in the company of a British agent he could pretend that he had baited a trap for the enemy and set the spring.

Arnold answered the challenge, identified himself, and the two officers rode on to Belmont. The American general officer commanding had himself escorted the British major through the American outposts.

No one can ever know all that happened at Belmont. For much of the time André and Arnold had no witness to their discussions and neither left an account, but as the terms for Arnold's treason had been settled substantially by correspondence, it can be assumed that some of the time was spent upon a clarification of the disposition of American forces around West Point and more upon a description by Arnold of the manner in which he had weakened his forces and fortifications. His habitually sardonic humor, the frustrations of several years, and the realization that he was at last close to tasting the twin delights of revenge and self-justification must have put Arnold into fine humor and good voice. He had moved his troops with considerable cunning so that each shift of strength could be justified to his own side even though it beckoned an easy way into West Point for an informed enemy. He had created a large gap in the fortress wall on the pretence of preparing the wall for repairs. Even, using the same excuse that repairs were needed, he had removed one of the links from the iron chain across the Hudson below West Point and had replaced it with a temporary link so weak that it would snap when struck by a ship under way.

All this and more Arnold must have told André, with frequent stabs of his finger at the maps and charts laid out before them. Dawn broke and soon there was enough light in the room to make the lamp ineffective. But still the final details of the British assault had not been settled and without that André's mission was incomplete.

Thus it was that when Smith hurried up to the house to try to bustle André away before all of them risked the full light of day he found the two men still urgent with conversation. They would continue their talk over breakfast.

And now, as so often in this story, accident played its part, tragically for André, benevolently for the new American nation.

For some weeks Colonel James Livingston, in command at Verplanck's Point, had been pressing Arnold to provide him with two heavy guns. Arnold, for reasons that are obvious, had refused, but the presence of *Vulture* within sight of his position so infuriated Livingston that he decided to mount a four pounder, and, without informing Arnold, persuaded Colonel Lamb, the artillery commander at West Point, to supply ammunition. This Lamb had done, but somewhat grudgingly.

> Firing at a ship with a four-pounder is, in my opinion, a waste of powder as the damage she will sustain is not equal to the expense.

As the light improved on the morning of September 22, Livingston's amateur gunners made their first attempt to prove wrong their professional colleague. Breakfast at Belmont was dramatically interrupted by the sound of gunfire. Smith, Arnold, and André rushed to the window. Not one of them can have been pleased to see *Vulture* slip her anchor and move off downstream, but the military men would have realized that Sutherland was doing no less than his duty in taking his ship out of range. (*Vulture* was in fact hit several times and Sutherland himself wounded slightly.) There was as yet no reason for undue tension, and yet from the moment when *Vulture* left her station a touch of panic settled upon the situation; and in consequence, two of the most experienced and courageous officers of the Revolutionary War launched themselves into a series of mistakes so elementary that they would have shamed children playing at soldiers.

André was still in his British uniform and Arnold without question the commanding officer of the area. Had he been concerned only for André's safety he could have escorted him back past the picket, provided him with a safe conduct and a flag of truce, found for him a boat, and sent him off after *Vulture*. It must have been likely that the whole affair would then come to the attention of Arnold's superiors, but he had never been slow to bluster or bluff his way out of difficult situations, and it can only be assumed that on this occasion two factors caused Arnold to lose his nerve and André his wits. The first was the knowledge that the boatmen who had brought André had already refused to take him back. The second was the obsessive determination, which both men shared, that nothing must be allowed to jeopardize their conspiracy. Rather than risk suspicion and therefore failure Arnold was prepared to venture André's life, and André was ready to accept handicaps that cold analysis after the event sees as both unnecessary and potentially suicidal.

Arnold insisted that he must hurry back to West Point. This was reasonable enough for his extended absence might well have aroused comment and even suspicion. But if André had to use the land route back to New York there was nothing to prevent him setting off forthwith or alternatively waiting for the comparative safety of another night. His chances were high of riding through the sparsely populated countryside without being noticed, and, even had he been challenged, given a safe-conduct in his own name signed by Arnold, it is more than likely that he would have been allowed to pass. At the very worst, he would have found himself a prisoner of war with a strong case to dispute his captors' right to hold him. Even with the safe-conduct that he did carry, in the name of John Anderson, the possibilities were good that he would not be held by an American outpost. But Arnold insisted that Smith find for André an American uniform, thereby submitting him to immediate delays, to the likelihood that those who were asked to fulfil such an extraordinary request might turn suspicious, and to the eventual danger that, if caught, André might well have sacrificed his right to claim prisoner-of-war status. André did protest against this proposal but Arnold was adamant and André conceded the point, comforting himself presumably with two related provisions of military etiquette: the first, that as he had been brought within the American lines by Arnold he was technically under Arnold's command and in effect already a prisoner of war; and the second, that although a prisoner may be punished for attempting to escape it is recognized by all armies that in making the attempt he is doing his duty and so the punishment is not generally severe, whatsoever disguise he may have adopted.

Arnold rode off to West Point and Smith went in search of the American uniform. It was midafternoon when he returned with the uniform. Instead, he gave to André a civilian greatcoat to wear over his regimentals.

There were still some hours of daylight left but both men were eager to be off.

Just before leaving Belmont, André crammed Arnold's plans of West Point into his riding boots.

Of all the mistakes of that day this was the most fatuous and, as such, is beyond explanation. Clinton had specifically ordered that André must not carry papers. André, an intelligence officer of rare skill, had had twelve hours to study the plans and to commit to mind the salient points. Even had he doubted his memory, which seems unlikely for André, he had had ample time to reduce the relevant information to coded notes or to a cypher sketch, the kind of thing which he had contrived a hundred times and more in the last few years. Instead, in the full knowledge that he was about to ride through uncertain country, he carried incriminating evidence which would have to be discovered if he were searched.

All went well on the first part of the ride. The two men and Smith's Negro servant crossed the Hudson at King's Ferry, then went north for a few miles before turning east at Peekskill. Several times on the way Smith exchanged greetings with passersby and twice he talked at some length with travelers who recognized him. But it was not until after dark, when they were almost clear of the country controlled by American forces, that they were challenged by a military unit, a patrol under Captain Ebenezer Boyd. Even then Smith's story and the safe-conduct for John Anderson convinced Boyd.

Boyd had a warning for the two riders. The middle zone between the two armies was always the hunting ground for "cowboys" and "skinners," deserters from both sides and criminals who had never belonged to either who took advantage of the absence of authority to prey upon outlying homesteads, unarmed travelers, and cattle drovers. In the last few days, villains of this kind had been more than ordinarily active, and because of this, Boyd advised Smith against traveling by night.

Smith was not difficult to convince; André was

persuaded only after some argument. The two men found lodging in the house of a Scotsman who had himself just suffered a cattle raid, and when they were on their way next morning and stopped at a farm for breakfast, they were once more reminded of Boyd's advice because the woman who fed them had lost most of her possessions to "skinners" only two days earlier.

As they rode on André threw off the unusual taciturnity that had gripped him since first he boarded *Vulture*. It was as if, now that he was coming close to the end of his journey with Smith, he were determined to leave his companion with a memory of the André that others knew, the André who had charmed Lichfield, Bath, the courts of Germany, the Quaker homes of Pennsylvania, the drawing rooms of Philadelphia, and the messes of the British army. He talked of the theater, books, art, and music. With one part of his mind, Smith listened and was appropriately fascinated. But the very ease of André's conversation brought Smith to the point of decision. The experience with Boyd had strengthened Smith's conviction that he could manage an American challenge, but the tales told last night by Boyd, the Scotsman, and the woman that morning worried him far more. Skinners and cowboys would not have any respect for a friend of General Arnold even if he were also the brother of the Loyalist chief justice of New York. And now Smith and André were virtually free from military challenge but about to move into the very heart of brigand territory. Surely this confident young officer riding at his side did not need Smith as guardian against cowboys or skinners.

Smith made up his mind. At Pine's Bridge where the road crossed the Croton River, Smith suddenly declared that he would not be going on to White Plains, as he had promised. André must ride on alone.

André took the announcement in good part, shook hands, and rode on toward Tarrytown. The morning was fine and the country magnificent. André kept his horse to a steady trot.

Once he passed an American officer riding alone toward West Point. For a second they glanced at each other; a look of puzzlement in the American's eye. André was well past before he realized that he had known the man, Colonel Webb of the Third Connecticut Regiment, a prisoner of war on parole, but he had no time to consider the miracle of his escape from recognition before he had to concentrate upon controling his horse as he approached a gimcrack bridge over a tiny stream.

Suddenly three men leaped out at him. One of them was wearing a British tunic, and in the confusion of the moment André thought that he had fallen in with a British patrol. With a sigh of relief he admitted that he was a British officer. They took no notice; their respect for both Britain and America was not equal to their greed for loot, and although André, unwashed, unshaven, and covered with dust, did not look much of a catch, his boots were unmistakably of good quality, and good boots were more valuable than gold. He was ordered to dismount.

André tried bribery. The offer of his gold watch convinced them that he was in fact a British officer, for few Americans carried anything so grand, but it also reinforced their covetousness and, at the same time, reduced to nothing the value of the pass from Arnold which he showed them. He was searched and in those handsome boots the three looters found Arnold's maps. Here were riches beyond boots or gold watches. They marched André off to the nearest American post, North Castle, where they handed him over to the commanding officer, Lieutenant Colonel John Jameson.

Again, the American nation had been saved by accident, and this time the agents of salvation were three villains who, had they been caught at their habitual pastimes by their countrymen, would have been hanged without hesitation. Instead, for their work on September 23, 1780, John Paulding, David Williams, and Isaac Van Wart, won for themselves fame as national heroes and, more important, pensions for life.

André was dejected. He realized that the conspiracy was close to ruin, but there was still a chance that he could bring about a last-minute success. If he could have himself and the papers delivered to Arnold they might yet fool the Americans. At all events it was his duty to do his best to warn Arnold, and, as for himself, even if the plot failed, there was no call for despair. He had been a prisoner of war before and had survived.

André presented to Jameson the safe-conduct in the name of John Anderson and demanded, that, if he were to be held, then at least the general who had signed the paper must be informed. The request was reasonable; indeed it was Jameson's plain duty to send not only a message but the prisoner himself to his superior, General Arnold, for interrogation. It took some time for Jameson to prepare his report, and as he wrote his eyes turned frequently to the maps that had been taken from the prisoner. It seems clear that he recognized Arnold's hand but, even so, did not come to suspect his commander. However, he did decide to prepare a separate report for General Washington, whom he knew to be somewhere in the vicinity of Danbury.

Jameson was not a quick worker. It was several hours before he ordered an escort to take André back to West Point. Lieutenant Solomon Allen, the messenger to Arnold, went with the party, but Jameson was still

working on his report for Washington half an hour later
when his second-in-command rode into North Castle.
Major Benjamin Tallmadge knew far more of secret
service matters than his superior. Like Jameson he
remembered Arnold's instructions about a Mr. John
Anderson but when he saw the plans on Jameson's table
he leaped immediately to the correct conclusion. Arnold
was somehow involved with the British. He begged
Jameson to recall Anderson so that they might themselves interrogate him.

So André was brought back to North Castle. But
neither Jameson nor Tallmadge thought to recall Allen.
Fortune that had turned so steadfastly against André at
this moment chose to favor Benedict Arnold.

Back at North Castle, André, having realized that he
had done all that he could for the conspiracy and for his
fellow conspirator, decided that the time had come to
look to his own safety and honor. Without shame he
admitted that he was Major John André, adjutant-general of the British army, and without shame he sat down to
write to General Washington.

The letter, which went eventually to Washington
with Jameson's report and Arnold's plans, rehearsed the
situation as André undoubtedly saw it. He did not name
Arnold. He had "agreed to meet upon ground not within
posts of either army" a person who was to give him
intelligence. Such arrangements were entirely appropriate to the code of warfare practiced by all armies. But
"against my stipulation, my intention and without my
knowledge beforehand, I was conducted within one of
your posts." From that moment he had considered
himself a prisoner of war, with both right and duty "to
concert my escape." He was concerned, and such as the
habit of the time genuine in his concern that Washing-

ton should not doubt the propriety of his behavior. But he was also a realist and as such not above reminding Washington that the British held a number of Americans accused of conspiracy though he modified the possibility that this could be taken as a threat by suggesting that these captives might be exchanged for him.

Meanwhile, at Robinson House, Arnold was waiting; his eagerness for news of André's safe return to New York was much increased by his knowledge that Washington was expected at West Point and with him Lafayette and Knox. His mind was not made any easier by the fact that his own aides chose the evening meal of September 24 as their moment to beard him about his friendship with Joshua Smith. That man, they said, was not trustworthy, and the general risked his own reputation by having Smith so often in his company.

The attack must have shaken Arnold but, had he only known it, the perfect reply was available to Arnold. At just the time when his subordinates were lambasting Arnold about his unreliable acquaintance, only fifteen miles away at Fishkill, Joshua Smith was sitting down to dinner with General Washington.

The history of the ten hours between the beginning of the two supper parties—at Robinson House and Fishkill on September 24—and the end of breakfast at Robinson House on September 25 is like a French farce from which most of the comedy has been removed. Characters bustled around a stage some 20 miles wide. Washington was in strange company; Arnold engaged on an embarrassing conversation. The messenger sent from Jameson to Washington missed him several times. Allen was taking a remarkably long time to get through to Arnold. Sutherland with *Vulture* was back at his old station off Tellers Point.

And, soon after dawn on September 25 the tempo of the tragi-comedy increased. At dawn Washington, who had the foxhunter's enthusiasm for early morning exercise and the habitual zeal among senior military men for making subordinates share in their pleasures, decided that he would ride to Robinson House for breakfast. A galloper was despatched to warn General and Mrs. Arnold. As Washington's headquarters was peripatetic, his secretary, Colonel Alexander Hamilton, had to supervise the loading of the baggage and before he left Fishkill, Washington, Lafayette, Knox, and their aides were already well on the road. As his party came opposite West Point, Washington changed his mind. He would like to inspect some of the positions on the east side of the Hudson. His companions must have shown some signs of disappointment as they realized that their long overdue breakfast was to be further delayed. Washington, pretending to misunderstand their looks, made one of his rare jokes: "I know you young men are all in love with Mrs. Arnold. Go take your breakfast with her, and tell her not to wait for me."

Lafayette and Knox were too senior to regard themselves as "young men" even for the love of Peggy Arnold and breakfast, but their aides rode off to give her the courteous part of Washington's message, but not the flattery.

Having arrived at the Robinson House, they were taken straight to the dining room to join Arnold. Peggy was in her room, adding a touch of artifice to her natural beauty in preparation for the arrival of the commander-in-chief and presumably telling her mirror that soon she would be welcoming another and perhaps livelier commander.

Arnold and the two aides began breakfast. Soon

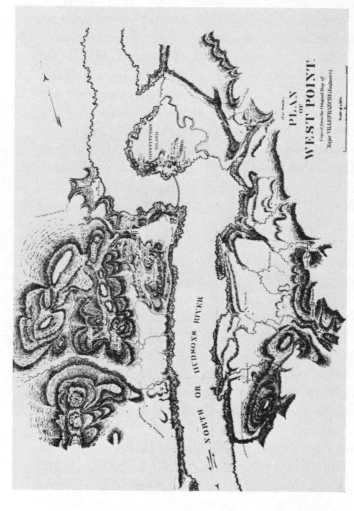

Plan of West Point on North or Hudson River as drawn by Major Villefranche. *Courtesy of the Department of the Army, Hq., U.S. Military Academy, West Point, New York.*

they were joined by Hamilton, and then, almost immediately, a servant came to tell Arnold that a despatch had arrived from Jameson.

He excused himself and in the hallway read the message that told him that his plot had been discovered and that his attempt to emulate General Monck had come only to disaster.

Arnold hobbled up the stairs, burst in on Peggy, and started to tell her that their conspiracy had failed and that he must escape before Washington arrived. Peggy fainted before he had got out one whole sentence. He left her lying on the floor, walked coolly into the dining room, announced that he had to go across to West Point on urgent business and that Mrs. Arnold was unwell. Then he hurried out of the house yelling for the coxswain of his barge and for a horse.

He galloped to the river, his coxswain running at his side, boarded the barge, and ordered the crew to row to *Vulture* some 18 miles downstream. They must hurry, he urged, because, when he had finished a parley with the British under a flag of truce, he must get back for a meeting with General Washington.

At about this moment Washington himself arrived at the Robinson House. Washington was not particularly surprised to find Arnold absent; it was only proper that a general should go about his duties even when his superior was expected, and it had been Washington not Arnold who had lingered by the way. He would have breakfast and then row over to the Point to find Arnold. He was suitably solicitous about Mrs. Arnold but did not ask to see her.

Peggy had in fact recovered in part from the first shock. Such private letters as she could find she destroyed, but she could not get at Arnold's official papers, for the day before one of his aides had been taken ill and was using the office as a sick room.

Once Washington had left, however, either her unnatural calm began to falter or else, and more probably, her natural cunning took control; either the lonely wife felt that she must have someone as confidant or else the practiced conspirator, realizing that her husband had had ample time to make his escape, decided that now it was up to her to establish for herself a new role as a wronged innocent. She went into a hysterical fit of repeating over and over again, at first in front of a servant, that Arnold had left her forever, that she was a widow, her child an orphan. The servant brought one of Arnold's official "family," Colonel Franks. Peggy repeated the performance, and Franks, who could not quite understand what she was saying but knew something of Peggy's tantrums and of the tempestuous quarrels that sometimes broke out between her and Arnold, promptly sent for a doctor.

Downstairs, Hamilton knew nothing of all this, but he was soon to have news far more shattering than a woman's hysterics. The messenger sent with the package containing Jameson's report for Washington and the papers taken from André had at last found his way to Robinson House. As Washington's secretary, Hamilton opened the package and in a few seconds he knew why Arnold had left and where he was going.

He must have contemplated giving the alarm but Hamilton had not risen so quickly in Washington's service by being susceptible to panic. It was more than likely that Arnold was already safe with the British. Hamilton's duty was to warn Washington and to avoid the spread of dismay in the army. Quietly, thoughtfully, he walked out of the house, mounted his horse, and rode off to look for the commander-in-chief.

He met Washington just as he reached the riverbank—a very angry Washington, who had spent two hours inspecting West Point and in that time had discovered much evidence, as he thought, of Arnold's dilatoriness and inefficiency. Succinctly Hamilton told Washington the news of Arnold's treachery and flight; then he handed to him the incriminating documents and the letter from André.

It was, perhaps, the greatest shock and the saddest that Washington had ever received, and his misery was in no way reduced by the necessity to remain outwardly calm. He had admired Arnold, and had defended him against powerful enemies. The very thought of treachery was anathema to Washington, but treason from this quarter was a national tragedy and, Washington knew, also a reflection on his judgment and potentially a menace to his prestige.

His loathing for the whole affair was increased when, later that day, he called on Peggy Arnold and found her still distraught. Like Hamilton, Knox, and Lafayette, who all followed him into Peggy's room, Washington was convinced that Arnold had betrayed not only his country but also his wife and child. His total revulsion added a dimension of hatred to Washington's determination to bring justice to those who had conspired and may help to account for the fact that in the end he allowed justice to be subverted into revenge.

5. Case for George Washington

WASHINGTON RAGED, but he did not forget his duties as a commander. Orders went immediately to West Point to have the garrison alerted and the defenses checked. General Greene was instructed to hurry up reinforcements. Reliable senior officers were sent to take charge of the outlying positions at Verplanck's Point, Stony Point, and King's Ferry. As for André, Washington was already close to judging his case before ever he had heard all the evidence. His instruction to have André brought to the Robinson House under heavy escort contained the ominous phrase "I would not wish Mr. André to be treated with insult, but he does not appear to stand upon the footing of a common prisoner-of-war and therefore he is not entitled to the usual indulgencies they receive."

Peggy Arnold raved, but it is more than likely that her ravings were carefully contrived. She wanted more than sympathy and the throwing-off of any suspicion that might associate her with the plot. She knew that the chances of joining her husband were for the moment slight, but she doubted that even she could for long maintain her act whilst under the constant observation of senior American officers and, if not New York with Arnold, then Philadelphia with her family was the next best thing.

It says much for Peggy's histrionic ability and little for the perspicacity of those she had helped to betray that all at West Point, including Washington, went out of their way to help her through her calamity. With time some came to mistrust her, but only by the inequitable standards of guilt by association, and almost 150 years would pass before the accusation of complicity could be settled upon her with certainty. True, one man who may have met her within days of the debacle did report that Peggy had boasted her part in the plot and had admitted to her bedroom "theatricals," but even Aaron Burr said nothing of all this until Peggy was dead, and no nineteenth-century American reader (and few nineteenth-century American historians) believed any story put out by a man who was himself a traitor and a notorious libertine.

Washington had probably made up his mind to send Peggy to Philadelphia, and as soon as possible, before ever he received a request to that end from a most unlikely source: Benedict Arnold.

Immediately upon reaching *Vulture*, even before Sutherland and Robinson could question him about poor André, Arnold sat down to write to Washington.

Sir: The heart which is conscious of its own rectitude, cannot attempt to palliate a step which the world may censure as wrong; I have ever acted from a principle of love to my country since the commencement of the present unhappy contest between Great Britain and the Colonies; the same principle of love to my country actuates my present conduct, however it may appear inconsistent to the world, who very seldom judge right of any man's actions.

I have no favor to ask for myself. I have too often experienced the ingratitude of my country to attempt it; but, from the known humanity of your Excellency, I am induced to ask your protection for Mrs. Arnold from every insult and injury that a mistaken vengeance of my country may expose her to. It ought to fall only on me; she is as good and as innocent as an angel, and is incapable of doing wrong. I beg she may be permitted to return to her friends in Philadelphia, or to come to me, as she may choose; from your Excellency I have no fears on her account, but she may suffer from the mistaken fury of the country.

I have to request that the enclosed letter may be delivered to Mrs. Arnold, and she be permitted to write to me.

I have also to ask that my clothes and baggage, which are of little consequence, may be sent to me; if required, their value shall be paid in money. I have the honor to be with great regard and esteem, your Excellency's most obedient humble servant.
Benedict Arnold.

N.B. In justice to the gentlemen of my family, Colonel Varick and Major Franks, I think myself in honor bound to declare that they, as well as Joshua Smith, Esq., (who I know is suspected) are totally ignorant of any transactions of mine, that they had reason to believe were injurious to the public.

Read even as part of history's miserable anthology of treason this is an extraordinary letter. Here is no Judas, wracked with guilt at what he has done; there is no penitence and scarcely any explanation except such as is hinted at by reminders of old grievances. Yet read in the context of Arnold's life it is by no means out of the ordinary but instead seems to epitomize his character.

"The heart which is conscious of its own rectitude" is in no need of confession or penitence. Even in the moment of his greatest failure Arnold looks into the mirror of his conscience and cannot there find any cause to blame himself for what has happened. His treason has not prospered but he will not call it treason because he defines words according to the dictionary of his own actions. He knows that others will brand him traitor but this is because they are lesser beings incapable of measuring his true motives. Almost, he launches into a new conspiracy, this time with Washington as his accomplice, for Washington is the one man for whom he has genuine esteem, the one man he knows to be his equal as a patriot, the one man whom he can accept as his peer in matters of honor and principle, the one man who can understand what he has done and why.

It is the letter of a megalomaniac.

But are there in it some signs of grace? Certainly not in the request for his clothes and possessions. Even if one measures Arnold by his own generous yardstick, as a man who had attempted to change the fate of a nation out of love for that nation, it is difficult to accept that, at this very time when his great purpose had been thwarted, he should be thinking about such trivialties. The pleas for his aides, and for Smith, have a more worthy air, but on analysis the worthiness vanishes. He knew that Washington would expect such protestations (especially for Peggy) and that without them all his claims to be a man of honor would be ridiculous. For Varick and Franks he could write with ease, for both could be proved innocent even according to the judgment of the multitude, "who very seldom judge right of any man's actions." Smith, he wanted out of American hands for two reasons. First, because Arnold was now entirely dependent upon the British, and if because of him and without any intervention on his part, the brother of the Loyalist chief justice of New York came to harm, his welcome in New York might well be even less warm than would be likely even for a failed traitor. Secondly, he could not be sure how much Smith knew or suspected about Peggy's role in the conspiracy and must have feared that even if he suspected nothing, under interrogation he might invent the truth. As for Peggy herself, although there can be no doubt that Arnold loved her deeply and wanted her safe, he realized, just as she had realized, that whilst she was under the close supervision of senior American officers she was always in danger of becoming a suspect. And Arnold realized, what Peggy may not have realized, that if she were held as a hostage, then he would be under pressure to give himself up and that such pressure might be applied by his own conscience and even by the British.

There remains a mystery: the omission from Arnold's letter of all mention of John André, the man who now stood in most danger. If Arnold was hoping to buy favor with the British by interceding on behalf of Smith, how much richer his reward if he had secured the release of the adjutant general. If Smith's captivity were a potential menace to Peggy's freedom, then how much greater (at least at first sight) the danger to her from André who most certainly did know of her involvement. If, by his crazy logic, Arnold's credibility with Washington depended on his going through the performance that would be expected of a man of honor, then why not attempt those actions for André? The Americans might not have accepted his admission that André had been in effect his prisoner, but Arnold could not forecast their action and it would have cost him nothing to try; and if

Self-portrait of John André, drawn while awaiting judgement.
Courtesy of Yale University Art Gallery.

he did not try, because he was equally uncertain of British attitudes, he must face the danger that as a hostage André was more valuable than Peggy. The Americans might be very willing to hand him over in exchange for Arnold and the British more than eager to accept the deal.

Romantic and gruesome speculation is insupportable that Arnold was deliberately revenging himself upon his wife's former lover, and there is no more evidence to bolster the theory that Arnold's malice sprang from his discomfort during their short meeting when the arrogant Arnold had suffered from the haughtiness of the British officer who despised both his Americanism and his treachery, that at Smith's house Arnold had discovered in André a blown-up example of all that sense of superiority that he had already suffered from his own colleagues.

The closest that one can come to explaining Arnold's failure to help André—and the best for his memory—must come once more from Arnold's obstinate conviction that he lived by the code of his time and understood that code. As a man of honor, he would expect others to be honorable. He would see that André was at risk, but he would expect Washington to be too honorable to consider him as anything but a prisoner of war. He would know that André, another man of honor, would never betray a woman, and that however tempted, Clinton's ethics would not allow him to surrender to certain death a reformed rebel.

If this is the explanation—and it is by no means watertight—then to it must be added the sardonic footnote that Arnold was right in all his judgments except about the man who time and his nation have chosen for reverence, George Washington.

Whatever Arnold's assessment of Washington's character, and whether that assessment was right or wrong, from the moment when Arnold reached *Vulture* the focus of attention must shift to Washington. Hitherto the major roles had been played by two actors, André and Arnold, each of them prepared by his background to represent a different interpretation of duty, the two of them moving inexorably to the moment of meeting. Now that Arnold had failed but was safe with the British and André had failed but was tragically unsafe among the Americans, both men lost their power of action. Thereafter only Washington could have changed the finale. André, Arnold, Clinton, Hamilton, everyone, both British and American who sought to influence the conclusion—all knew that they must address themselves to Washington.

From now on all depended on Washington and his notion of duty and loyalty. The tiny humans with their emotions, charm, passion, and fallibility were brushed aside, and the Olympian took over. Washington, stern, unshakable by sentiment and utterly dedicated to the cause of which he was both leader and representative, was now the only arbiter.

When Clinton heard the news of André's capture the personal shock thrust from his mind even the disappointment at the failure of his great venture. He wrote to Washington, rehearsing the argument that André was *de facto* a prisoner of war and that, even if he were found to be *de jure* (and only by some fine point of law) a spy, still there were extenuating circumstances and even in war civilized conventions which must protect him from the utmost consequences of espionage.

On the American side, Washington's official family, and notably Alexander Hamilton, turned advocate for

André and pestered their commander with pleas for clemency.

The American army at large had been stunned by the news of Arnold's attempted treason and defection. He had always had his enemies, had done his best to add to their number by his arrogance, and had suffered a steady increase to their number because of the stories, justified and unjustified, about his greed. But few had doubted his bravery, and in the minds of most of his contemporaries courage was substantially equated with honor. Most American fighting men had long since lost the emotional antipathy to their British opponents that Sam Adams had engendered in the days of the Boston Massacre. They would shoot them down in battle but recognized that the British officer and soldier no less than the American was performing his own uncomfortable duty by the lights of his conscience and according to the dictates of his government. Even, if they tried very hard to be reasonable, most of the more educated in the Continental Army could find some understanding for the stance of the Tories and especially for those Tories who had the courage to fight for their convictions. But treason was repugnant to them all, and treason in a man who had been from time to time a national hero was shattering.

Yet none of the repugnance for Arnold rubbed off on his fellow conspirator. In captivity André recovered all the charm that had won him admiration and affection in happier times. Before, when he had been a prisoner in Pennsylvania, he had been the favorite of his jailers, and now, again a prisoner, he worked the magic of his personality on all who had him in charge. Even that fiery cavalryman, Major Tallmadge, who had commanded of the escort that took André first to West Point and then to his ultimate prison at Mabie's Tavern. Tappan, and who had little doubt that André would be judged a spy, was deeply affected. Later he wrote: "It often brought tears to my eyes to find him so agreeable in conversation on different subjects, when I reflected on his future fate and that, too, as I feared, so near at hand."

Washington, almost alone, was unmoved. Although he was never more than 20 miles from his prisoner he never met him, did not reply to André's request for an interview, and turned away from every suggestion made by his officers that he should see André. Such was his adamance that it seems almost as if he were nervous lest the famous charm might work to disrupt even his resolution. For resolution it was, carefully considered and carried out with the impassivity of a marble statue. That Washington was wounded in his spirit by Arnold's treachery there can be no doubt, and perhaps as has been suggested, the hurt was intensified by his sympathy for the pretty and wronged wife of the traitor. Some commentators, who have thought that Washington's attitude to André needed justification beyond the defense of legality, have claimed that he had it in mind to be revenged upon the British for the execution of Nathan Hale, but Hale was an ineffective spy whose only claim upon history and Washington's recollection was his ringing gallow's speech: "I only regret that I have but one life to lose for my country." Emotion of one sort or another may have touched Washington, but Hamilton, who knew him better than most, knew also why he was implacable and imperturbable in his prosecution of André. It was, Hamilton said, "hard hearted policy." Washington's cause had been threatened, and he was by no means sure that there were not more threats to come. His authority had been put at risk, and he had to

Portrait of General George Washington by Charles Wilson Peale. *Courtesy of Mount Vernon Ladies' Association.*

demonstrate that it was unassailable. Because he revered the cause and believed that it might collapse if his authority were seen to waver, he turned away from the possibility of mercy and held to the severity of the law. The lesson that he had it in mind to read was intended as much for his own army and for sniping congressmen as for the British. That lesson must be read with dramatic effect and quickly; before the British could find an effective counterstroke, before the clamor of American voices pleading for clemency could reach such a frenzy as to be of itself dangerous to his authority, and perhaps (as one almost hopes) before Washington, the man of humane qualities, could take over from Washington, the austere leader and commander.

On September 29 Washington called together a board of officers to examine André carefully and "as speedily as possible to report a precise state of his case, together with your opinion of the light in which he ought to be considered and the punishment that ought to be inflicted."

This board has often been called a court and the investigation in the Dutch Church at Tappan is more often than not referred to as the "trial of Major André." It was nothing of the sort and by the custom of war, then as now, there was no reason why it should be. Within the limitations prescribed by convention a commander-in-chief has almost entire responsibility for the fate of prisoners of war and spies. The board summoned to Tappan had no authority to do more than report to Washington. At the hearing André had no prisoner's friend, no witnesses were called, and André's evidence was not taken on oath—all divergencies from the practices of courts-martial. Had this been a court-martial, André would have faced a number of officers of his own rank under the presidency of a senior officer. Instead he stood before almost every general officer that could be brought to Tappan in the time available. The president of the board was Washington's senior general, Nathanael Greene, and the legal adviser, the Judge Advocate-General John Lawrence. Washington was committing all his senior colleagues; more, he was demonstrating to the army, to the British, and to Congress the unanimity of his commanders.

(It is not without relevance to the confusion of loyalties that prevailed during the Revolutionary War that, of the 14 generals on the board, one was a German, one a Frenchman, and three had been born in Britain, as was also the judge advocate general.)

The proceedings of the board were brief and conducted with ineffable courtesy. At one point a chance remark of Greene's was interpreted by André as an attempt to trap him into incriminating Arnold. With dignity he refused to be drawn and the president of the board apologized.

As so often before, André's personality was exercising an influence on his audience. The members of the board came to look upon him with respect and almost with affection. But if the charm were undiminished even by the delicacy of the circumstances and the courage unshaken by the awareness of his situation, as an advocate in his own case André was ineffective. He was too honest. When questioned about the flag of truce that was said to have been on the boat that brought him from *Vulture*, instead of insisting that it had been there, which at very worst would have set his word against the word of the boatmen, or pretending that he had not noticed, or that he could not remember, which would have put doubt into the minds of the board members, he admitted that there had been no flag. (This whole episode of the flag of truce is one of the unresolved mysteries of the story. André, the one man who could have benefited from its existence, denied that there had been a flag. Not only Arnold, whose word must be suspect, but Sutherland and Robinson, who were men of honor, were prepared to swear on oath that it was flying when André left *Vulture*. The board did not question the boatmen.) When shown a letter written by him as John Anderson to Gustavus, arranging to meet at Dobbs Ferry, he admitted that it was his but added that he could not use it in his defense because, even though it did prove that he had never intended to enter the American lines, it was written from New York when he was under the command of Clinton.

Such frankness was natural to André but he may have made also a conscious decison that frankness was his surest shield. Like Arnold (but with far more reason) certain of his own rectitude, he may have decided that his case would be weakened if the board caught him in any attempt to dissemble or prevaricate, and he must have been convinced that, even were he found technically guilty, the death sentence would be averted either by the recommendation of the board or through the clemency recommendation of Washington.

After André had been returned to his prison the board listened as the judge advocate read letters from Clinton, Arnold, and Robinson. All three insisted that André had landed under a flag of truce, and as André had conceded that this was not so, such limited effectiveness as the letters might have had was virtually erased.

The nature of the proceedings at the Dutch Church set for the members of the board some tantalizing problems of conscience. Because their activities were circumscribed by Washington's instructions and because the responsibility for eventual decision rested entirely upon the commander-in-chief, the board members could content themselves with simple and direct advice to Washington, without becoming obsessed with the need to justify their conclusions. But, because they were not, in the strictest sense, a court of law, they were freed from the necessity to adhere to any strict rules of procedure or evidence. They could, for example, take into consideration not only the letters from Clinton, Robinson, and Arnold but also André's own letter to Washington written on September 24. (One of the explanations for André's somewhat incomplete and indecisive defense before the board may well be that he considered that much of it had already been covered by his letter.) If they so chose they were in a position to make their recommendations according to the principles of humanity rather than by any tenets of law or precedent; though were they to do so, still they might be overruled by Washington. Among men who were fighting for a cause that stood for equity, the temptation must have been great to use the principle of equity to save an attractive enemy, and there were undoubtedly some on the board who hoped to devise some means of saving an honest Englishman from suffering for the villainies of a dishonest American. However, whether by instinct or instruction it is impossible to tell, the board members knew what was expected of them and the judge advocate general's summary made any other verdict impossible. Lawrence was not notably antipathetic to André, but his cool assessment of the case, though some points in it might have been argued and even demolished by a defense counsel, was damning beyond escape.

Lawrence accepted that in law and in military custom there was no crime in an attempt to suborn a hostile general but that it would render all military organization superfluous could that very general serve as guardian to his own tempter. This reduced to nothing the value of Arnold's safe-conduct and to some extent made irrelevant the differences about the flag of truce. From the beginning André had acted under a false name and, in Lawrence's opinion, this too defiled both the pass and the flag. André had insisted, and no one denied, that he had entered the American lines in uniform but again, according to Lawrence, this was nullified by his false name, in itself a form of disguise, and therefore the civilian greatcoat was an irrelevance, at most a deepening of a disguise that already existed. Lawrence does not appear to have dealt with André's contention that, once he was taken past the sentry, he regarded himself as a prisoner of war, but presumably he felt that this too was nullified by Arnold's status as a traitor and by André's self-proclaimed *persona* as a civilian called John Anderson.

The verdict of the board was unanimous. André was a spy and as such he must die.

They had done their duty and would do no more. Even, they felt that they could do no more. But these were men of sensibility and even in public in the eighteenth century, feelings were not always disciplined by conventions. Greene wept as he signed the report. Lafayette later described his part in the verdict as "one of the most painful duties he had to perform." Even the lawyer, Lawrence, shuffled out a few uneasy words about a recommendation for mercy and broke off in midsentence, gulping down his tears. Von Steuben spat out a more comfortable phrase with which all could agree: "Would to God the wretch who drew him to death could have suffered in his place."

Away from the board and before the verdict was

announced, others were thinking the same thought and were acting on it. Several American slipped messages to the British suggesting that Arnold and André be exchanged, among them Washington's own secretary, Alexander Hamilton, who himself came close to treason in his secret efforts on behalf of the victim of Arnold's treachery.

It was all futile. Clinton, though deeply concerned for his friend and favorite staff officer, could not bring himself to break the military code by handing over a deserter to certain death. Further, however much his instinct might have persuaded him to despise Arnold's treachery, his reason insisted that Arnold was no traitor but a one-time rebel who had returned to his proper allegiance; and as a commander, Clinton appreciated, correctly, that Washington's difficulties were not ended just because Arnold's plot had been discovered. Others, even in the Continental Army in the North, were contemplating defection, and the army in the South was close to mutiny. If Clinton surrendered Arnold, he would surrender also the chance to encourage disaffection among Washington's followers.

Clinton had thought of other possibilities. He had been notably humane in his treatment of prisoners, a fact that even Washington had admitted, but now he was tempted to point out that he held many Americans whose offenses made them liable to the death penalty. He could threaten massive reprisals if André were executed and went so far as to draft a hectoring letter to Washington, but wiser counsel persuaded him that action of this kind would not deter the American, would make useful propaganda against the British that would help to rally to the Revolutionary cause even many who were fainthearted supporters, and could only lead to a crescendo of acts of brutality from both sides. The letter was never sent.

But several letters of various kinds were being hurried between the two headquarters. Washington wrote to Clinton informing him of the board's findings and of his decision to confirm the verdict and to order that André be executed on the very next day. On Clinton's behalf, Robinson wrote asking for permission for André's soldier-servant to go to Tappan. Permission was granted, and Peter Laune set off immediately carrying with him a clean uniform. Clinton himself prepared another draft letter setting forth the British arguments and persuaded Arnold to write an explanation which supported the view that André should be regarded as having acted under his orders. (The letter contained also Arnold's resignation from Washington's Army!) But the noblest and most tragic letter of all was written by André himself on the early morning of the day that he thought would be his last.

The decision of the board and Washington's immediate confirmation had been conveyed to André by the two enemy officers who in the time of his disaster had become his close friends, Hamilton and Tallmadge. André's self-control was more firm than either of the Americans could manage. Only two considerations shook his magnificent imperturbability. The fate of a spy was death on a gallows; this was no way for a man of honor to die. Surely Washington would allow him the end of a soldier by a bullet. Surely he would unbend so far as to order a firing squad instead of a rope. And, his second cause for horror, Clinton's feelings:

He has been lavish of his kindness, I am bound to him by too many obligations and love him too well, to bear the

thought that he should reproach himself, or other should
reproach him . . . I would not for the world, leave a
sting in his mind that should embitter his future days.

Could he be allowed to write a letter of reassurance to his
general?

Hamilton and Tallmadge were in tears. Hamilton
undertook to carry to Washington André's letter pleading
for a firing squad and to intercede with Washington on
both counts, and on both counts he was optimistic.
Washington permitted the letter—there was no reason in
policy or in law why he should not—but on the manner
of André's execution he was unrelenting. The reason is
clear: were he to allow André's death to be treated as
anything but the punishment of a spy, not only would he
open the way to doubts about the justice of the
condemnation, but also he would throw into question
his own determination, his own authority, and he would
reduce the efficacy of the lesson that he meant to read to
halfhearted friends and full-throated enemies.

Whether Washington's rigidity was justified even as
a matter of policy is for conjecture. An act of total
clemency might have served his purposes just as
effectively as severity, for it is possible that it would have
persuaded American opponents that he was certain of
his strength, and it might have embarrassed the British
no less than it pleased them, for it would have put them
in Washington's debt. As for the minor act of mercy
involved in allowing to André the death of a soldier, it is
difficult to see how this could have weakened anything
but Washington's reputation for austerity.

By refusing to relent in the slightest degree, except
by sending André breakfast from his own table,
Washington almost outreached himself. Hamilton was
so offended by this seemingly unnatural sternness that

he had doubts about continuing as a member of the official family. These doubts were admittedly short lived, but it is possible that they were strangled not by forgiveness but by the more congenial excitements that came to Hamilton in that winter of 1780 as he prepared for his marriage to Elizabeth Schuyler. Tallmadge too was incensed and did not keep his disgust to himself so that for a short time British intelligence thought that they might have here another Benedict Arnold.

But among the generality on the American side, although sympathy for André was almost universal, few criticized the decision to condemn him and, except those who were in personal contact with the prisoner, none doubted that as he had been found to be a spy so as a spy he must die.

It is a comment upon the unusual circumstances of the André case that even when the news of Washington's decision came formally to General Clinton's council, and though all present were naturally moved by André's fate and not unnaturally incensed by Washington's refusal to act mercifully, two members of the council did give it as their opinion that the Americans were acting within the strict interpretation of the law and of convention in treating André as a spy. (As with the board that had sat under Greene so also with Clinton's council there is revealed the confusion of loyalties in a time of civil war. Four councillors were American born and one German.)

To this same council meeting Clinton read André's last letter. The emotional strain was almost more than the general could bear. He stumbled over the words:

Your Excellency is doubtless already appraised of the manner in which I was taken [wrote André] and possibly

of the serious light in which my conduct is considered;
and the rigorous determination that is impending.

Under the circumstances, I have obtained General
Washington's permission to send you this letter; the
object of which is, to remove from your breast any
suspicion that I could imagine I was bound by your
Excellency's orders to expose myself to what has
happened. . . . I am perfectly tranquil in mind, and
prepared for any fate, which an honest zeal for my King's
service may have devoted me. . . . "

At this point in his reading Clinton began to sob and the
next words were hardly audible to his councillors:

In addressing myself to your Excellency on this occasion,
the force of all my obligations, and of the attachment and
gratitude I bear you, recurs to me. With all the warmth of
my heart, I give you thanks for your Excellency's profuse
kindness to me; and I send you the most earnest wishes
for your welfare, which a faithful, affectionate, and
respectful attendant can frame. . . . "

Clinton recovered sufficiently to read with clarity
André's pleas that his commission might be sold for the
benefit of his mother and three sisters who were
themselves suffering financially as a result of the
American war. (Commissions normally ended with the
death of the holder.) He enunciated tonelessly André's
tribute to the kindliness of those who held him captive,
then collected himself and in pride and full voice read
out André's still proud subscription: "John André,
Adjutant-General."

Grief gave way once more to anger. Again Clinton
was tempted to write a peremptory letter to Washington
warning him of the consequences to some Americans
held by the British if André was executed. Even he

thought to point out that Henry Laurens, the president of Congress, was held in the Tower of London. But the council advised against such actions and urged instead that some of their number go to Washington to argue the case.

A messenger was sent off immediately asking that a delegation consisting of the governor, lieutenant governor, and chief justice of New York (General James Robertson, Andrew Eliot, and William Smith) be granted a safe-conduct so that they could "meet your Excellency, or such person as you may appoint, to converse with them on the subject . . . and to declare to you my sentiments and resolutions."

This was a request that Washington could scarcely refuse unless he was prepared to abandon his own insistence that all that he did was according to the usages of war, but he remained adamant that he himself would stay aloof from the discussions. He also refused to allow all three to come through the American lines, perhaps because he did not want to offer even tacit recognition to the whole upper hierarchy of Loyalist New York but more likely because he wished to exclude particularly William Smith, brother of the man who was being held for trial in the same cause as André's. Robertson was a British general; he alone could come, and Greene could go to meet him.

Washington's acceptance of Clinton's suggestion made inevitable the postponement of André's execution.

There was a flicker of optimism among those who guarded André and who had become his firmest friends, admirers, and advocates. André himself, who was playing the greatest role of his life, must have found the strain of hope almost more unbearable than the fear of death. He had insisted that he was no hero, but he had been managing a convincing imitation. The fear of showing fear is a remarkably effective spur to courage; without it no battles could be fought for all armies would be in headlong retreat. But few men have been called upon to stay calm in such circumstances as those in which André found himself, cut off from his friends, convicted of a crime for which he could feel no guilt, and expecting an end that he could but regard as disgrace as well as death. Even the friendliness of his guards must have added to the temptation to reduce this inner tension by allowing himself the comfort of their pity. But André stayed emotionally erect, chatted easily with Hamilton and the other Americans, inspected his uniform with his soldier-servant. When he was alone, he busied himself with making a pen-and-ink self-portrait— the grimly determined effort of a man who would not let his spirit flinch nor allow his hand to be seen to shake, or was it the last reminder to history from a man who had hoped to have so much opportunity to make his name and his face famous?

If he had any thoughts that Robertson's mission would bring him a last-minute reprieve he does not appear to have talked of them with any of the Americans around him. They, for their part, must have known that Washington would not be deflected from his purpose except, perhaps, by the one slim chance that even Washington himself hoped that there might come from the meeting between Robertson and Greene the exchange of Arnold for André.

Greene's instructions from Washington were in fact explicit. He was to treat with Robertson as a gentleman but not as an officer: "the Case of an acknowledged Spy admitted no official Discussion" and "the Army must be satisfied by seeing Spies executed."

Robertson was a hardheaded Scot who did not give

up easily and who, when he thought he saw an opportunity to shame his adversary into his arguments, did not find it necessary to cloak his case with courteous diplomacy. "I said no Military Casuist in Europe would call André a Spy; and I would suffer Death myself if Monsieur Rochambault or General Knyphausen would call him by that name." Later Robertson put into more refined terms this blatant insinuation that the Americans were uncivilized when compared with their European allies, urging that "disinterested Gentlemen of Knowledge in the Law of War and Nations might be asked their Opinion on the Subject."

The conference between the two generals lasted for several hours. Greene could not accept the notion of arbitration by foreign officers and was in no position to go beyond his very limited instructions. Over and over again he returned to the point that the army must have its victim, and over and over again he fell back on André's "confession." He insisted that the only way out of this was for the British to hand over Arnold. ("This," according to Robertson, "I answered with a look only, which threw Green into Confusion.") And Robertson was no fool. Not only was he convinced that Greene did not like his instructions—"the Task was imposed and did not proceed from his own Thought—" but he was also convinced that Greene would argue the case with Washington as strenuously as Robertson had argued it with Greene. Late on the afternoon of October 1 Robertson wrote to Clinton, "I am persuaded André will not be hurt. Believe me."

He had not reckoned with the. awe in which Washington was held, even by his most senior officers. A few, a very few young hotheads like Alexander Hamilton would dare that gritty wrath; Lafayette had some especial relationship which allowed him on occasion to tease the commander-in-chief, but Greene was almost as austere as Washington and yet a subordinate. He had listened as he had been told and now he made his report on his meeting with Robertson clearly, honestly but without passion. He had offered an exchange and the British had refused.

The execution of John André was ordered for noon on October 2. That morning Alexander Hamilton sat down to write to his fiancée:

> Poor André suffers today. Everything that is amiable in virtue, fortitude, in delicate sentiment and accomplished manners, pleads for him, but hardhearted policy calls for a sacrifice. He Must die. I send you my account of Arnold's affair: and to justify myself to your sentiments, I must inform you that I urged compliance with André's request to be shot; and I do not think it would have had an ill-effect, but some people are only sensible to motives of policy and sometimes, from a narrow disposition, mistake it.
>
> When André's tale comes to be told, and present resentment is over, the refusing him the privilege of choosing the manner of his death will be branded with too much obstinacy.
>
> It was proposed to me to suggest to him the idea of an exchange for Arnold, but I knew I would have forfeited his esteem by doing it, and therefore declined it. As a man of honor, he could not but reject it, and I would not for the world have proposed to him a thing which must have placed me in the unenviable light of supposing him capable of meanness, or of feeling myself the impropriety of the measure. I confess to you, I had the weakness to value the esteem of a dying man, because I reverenced his merit.

On that fall morning André was called upon for the greatest histrionic performance of his life. Breakfast came as usual with the compliments of General Washington. He ate plentifully and with evident relish, turning every now and then from the table to talk with the ensign who had been assigned the duty of serving as his immediate guard. The sad experience was proving too much for the poise of the young American who was close to unmilitary hysteria. Like a senior officer holding his inexperienced subordinates from panic before their first battle André worked to keep the young man calm. He asked about the boy's family, gossiped about girls and dancing, about London and New York, about anything that came into his mind except that one grim thought that must have been with him all the time; the minutes ticking away toward noon.

After breakfast André's soldier-servant came to help him bathe, shave, and dress in his best uniform but without spurs or sword.

Other officer-guards arrived, and then Tallmadge and Hamilton. All this courtesy to his beloved master, the man they were about to murder, was beyond the logic of the British private soldier. He sobbed and between his sobs, using that most audible whisper which is the peculiar skill of the ordinary fighting man when close to his superiors, he muttered wondrous obscenities about the parentage, behavior, and future prospects of all Americans. Gently, smilingly, as to a favorite child who is behaving badly, André rebuked him, "Not in front of strangers."

Then the moment came. Picking up his hat André bowed to the American officers. "I am ready at any moment, gentlemen, to wait on you."

They moved out into the brisk morning. André,

erect but pale, took his place between two subalterns,
behind him marched his servant. There was a 40-man
escort, and at the head of the solemn procession a
drummer and four fife-players.

The eighteenth century loved a public execution as
much as the twentieth century a game of football, but
this was different. Despite the remoteness of Tappan a
considerable crowd lined the mile-long route up the hill
from Mabie's Tavern to the place of execution; and in
the crowd there were hundreds of officers and men from
Washington's army. They had not come to gloat and
certainly not to jeer. "No one refrained from proclaim-
ing his sympathy." From time to time André would
recognize someone among the crowd and would ask the
procession to stop so that he coud talk "with a friend."
Once he commented on the excellent quality of the
music.

On the last stretch of the awful march, and without
orders, Tallmadge took the place of one of the escorting
subalterns.

André had received from Washington no reply to his
request that if he must die it should be by firing squad;
and none had dared to tell him that no relaxation of the
sentence had been ordered. But somehow André had it
firmly in mind that at the last he would be treated as a
soldier. As he turned the final bend he saw the gibbet
and then, for the first time, his tightly held equanimity
was shattered. He stumbled, his fists clenched and
unclenched, and sweat broke out on his forehead.

Embarrassed into tactlessness one of the subalterns
asked, "Why this emotion, sir?" André answered, "I am
reconciled to my fate, but not to its mode," and then he
turned to Tallmadge, "Must I then die in this manner?"
Tallmadge, deeply stirred by sorrow for André and by

anger against those who had persisted in what he regarded as unnecessary heartlessness, could only nod. "How hard is my fate," said André, "but it will soon be over."

The gallows stood in full view of the house where Washington had made his headquarters. There all the blinds were drawn, perhaps as a token of mourning but perhaps because Washington did not care to look out upon the scene. Other senior officers, Greene among them, were gathered at the place of execution.

The panoply of doom was macabre and the scenario of the final tragedy long drawn out. A baggage wagon was placed under the gibbet, and on the wagon a black coffin. As André stepped forward to climb to this grisly platform, one of the attendant officers drew attention to some shortcoming in the preparations. The unseemly bustle that followed once more threatened André's composure. He controlled his emotions by concentrating on a round stone which he kicked from foot to foot. Then he shook hands with Tallmadge and, in a gesture as rare as it was courageous, threw his arm round the shoulders of his servant. No longer could he reprove the man for lack of respect to his betters nor hold him from shaming the British army in front of its enemies. This was the last true countryman that he would ever see, his last old friend. Now they were equals and it was the soldier who needed help. Strengthened by André's sympathy, the man made a superhuman effort, throttled his sobs, straightened his back, and stood firmly at atttention as if on the barrack square.

Now once more André stepped forward. His face was pale and his disgust as he clambered up on to his own coffin was so obvious that some who watched felt as if they "had been whipt." Calmly André took off his hat,

untied his cravat, and opened his shirt. The appointed
hangman, a Tory prisoner who had been promised his
freedom in exchange for his participation in this
unhappy event, stood by ready with the rope. Hampered
by his nervousness and by the black grease with which he
was covered in order to preserve his anonymity, he
bungled his first attempt to place the noose over André's
head. Gently, André pushed him away, set the rope
about his own neck, adjusted it carefully, then took a silk
handkerchief from his pocket and blindfolded himself.

The adjutant general read out the order for
execution and told André that he might speak. He
pushed the blindfold from his eyes and for the first time
that day looked directly at Greene and his companions.
He bowed low and, in a clear voice, said, "All I request of
you, gentlemen, is that you will bear witness to the world
that I die like a brave man." Only those close to him
heard his last words, "It will be but a momentary pang."

But even now the scant comfort of speed was denied
him. Once more some unnaturally officious attendant
noticed that not all the formalities had been completed.
The doomed man's arms must be tied behind his back.
The executioner shuffled forward with a piece of rope.
Again André shrugged him off. From his pocket he took
a second silk handkerchief. Ostentatiously he flicked at
the mark left by the man's hand on his uniform sleeve,
then handed the handkerchief to the executioner.

A drummer beat a tattoo, then one harsh beat. The
wagon was driven from under the gibbet. John André
had paid the price for Benedict Arnold's treason.

6. Aftermath

"THE TEARS OF thousands consecrated the spot where André lay." Thus, an American commentator on his countrymen's reaction to the death of the "amiable spy." On the other side the tragic news spread fast, and much of the army had donned mourning bands before the official instruction to do so was issued by Clinton's headquarters. Such was the indignation which mingled with the grief that, had Clinton ordered instead an immediate and general advance on West Point he would have found officers and other ranks more than ordinarily eager for the fight. Some, among his staff officers, recommended just such a course, and not only because they sensed that the army was tight sprung for revenge, not just because they suspected that Washington had not yet had time to repair all the mischief wrought in the West Point defenses by Arnold, but also because they believed that Washington's harshness toward André might have encouraged some of his followers to turn away from his leadership.

Clinton did nothing. He had never been a notably energetic general, and his hopes of outmaneuvering Washington had been centered for the most part on diplomatic and conspiratorial rather than bellicose planning. Hence, his rich ambition for the Arnold conspiracy. But Clinton's inactivity after he received the news of André's execution was not the result of disappointment—that was to come later and with it the enduring conviction that because of Arnold's failure he had been robbed of a place among the immortals of British military history. In the days that followed the return of André's servant with the sad news of his master's death, Clinton was in shock: for a dearly loved young friend, for a loyal staff officer, for a hero whom he had sent to his death.

Not so General Washington—the man who had actually condemned André—for him the closing of the blinds at his house at Tappan seems to have been a deliberate and symbolic gesture. Justice had been done and political necessity satisfied; now the whole affair could be shut off from public or private inspection. Others on both sides in the struggle might continue to debate the case. Hamilton's criticism of Washington's "harshness" was not silenced. General von Steuben, on the other hand, defended both Washington's condemnation of André and the manner of André's execution: "André was a spy, and in the Army was any other death than by the gibbet awarded to a spy?" Washington said nothing. Only once in all the rest of his days did he so much as mention the André case and then in a reply to Anna Seward's hysterical condemnation:

Remorseless Washington! the day shall come
Of deep repentance for this barbrous doom!

Then he rested his case (it must be admitted to Anna Seward's satisfaction) entirely on the offer made to exchange André for Arnold. Yet on another and not dissimilar issue—the case of a British officer chosen at random from among those captured at Yorktown

sentenced to death as an act of reprisal for the murder of
some Americans and reprieved only through the
intervention of the French—even several years after the
event Washington was hot (and inaccurate) in defense of
his honor and reputation for just dealing.

But, immediately after the death of André, Washington's aloofness was unreal. For him the Arnold affair
could not end with André dangling on a rope, and
Washington knew it. There was still the possibility that
the British would retaliate, and already before André's
death there were threats hanging over the South
Carolinians captured at Charleston and accused of
conspiracy. Washington wrote to Clinton inquiring
about their fate, and back came Clinton's reply.

Clinton was persuaded that it is "for the Interest of
Mankind that a Correspondence should exist between
Generals Commanding Adverse Armies." What
happened in Charleston was for Cornwallis to decide.

> But as I am well acquainted with Lord Cornwallis's
> Humanity, I cannot entertain the least Apprehension
> that he will stain the Lustre of the King's Arms by acts of
> Cruelty. The Friends of those Persons under the
> Description you give of them need be under no fear for
> their Safety. Lord Cornwallis is incapable of straining the
> Laws to take away the Lives or Liberties of the Innocent.
> If any forced Construction be put upon the Laws by his
> Lordship, it will be in favor of the Accused; and every
> Plea their Friends can offer for them will be humanely
> heard and respected.

As Washington in his request so Clinton in his reply
does not mention André, yet every phrase in Clinton's
letter carries an indictment of Washington's behavior to
his prisoner. Stern with military dignity, quivering with

humane indignation, writing this letter must have given to Clinton the few moments of release in these his darkest days.

And, though André was dead and Arnold safe with the British, for Washington the case could not be closed until a decision was taken about another participant in the conspiracy, Joshua Hett Smith.

On the day after André's appearance before General Greene and his board of officers another investigation began, also at Tappan. Smith was not a soldier but unlike André he was given the full process of a court-martial. The scrupulous manner of Smith's trial, the latitude that he was allowed in his own defense by the president of the court, the thoroughness with which witnesses were sought out and cross questioned by both prosecution and defense, the duration of the proceedings (almost four weeks), and the final verdict—all serve to heighten the contrast with the treatment of André and to strengthen the possibility that Hamilton was right when he asserted that André was the victim of policy not justice. Much of the evidence that was forthcoming at Smith's trial would have had considerable bearing on the case of Major André. And Smith's defense rested in part on the same premise that André had pleaded in the brisk process permitted to him: that he had been acting under Arnold's orders. Admittedly Smith could go beyond André, and the decision of the court that Smith be found not guilty because he had not known Arnold's treacherous intentions could not have been passed on André.

André had been unfortunate and had been served with less than justice; Smith was given every possible legal consideration and, even so, the impression must remain that he was fortunate in his judges. The verdict did not please his contemporaries and cannot satisfy history. Yet the manner in which Washington refused to abide by the decision of the court which he himself had convened adds weight to the suspicion that, because of his attitude to André, is almost a conviction: that Arnold's treachery had so disrupted Washington's generally unshakable equanimity as to deprive him of his habitual integrity. He refused to confirm the findings of the court and had Smith held a prisoner for several months, unaware of his ultimate fate, while he pondered the possibilities of handing Smith to the civil authority for a new trial. Eventually, the possibility of decision was taken away from Washington. Smith escaped.

Long before that happened Washington had left New York State. The army in the South was suffering at the skillful hands of Lord Cornwallis, pessimism was rife, and not a little disaffection. The unifying and indomitable presence of the commander-in-chief was needed in his native Virginia.

In her native Philadelphia Peggy Arnold was unwelcome. Already before André's execution the city's press had inferred that she had been party to the conspiracy. Almost immediately a campaign of vilification was directed not only against her but, conveniently at a time when the Revolution needed some whipping-boys and whipping-girls, against all those who had fraternized with the enemy during the British occupation. The Executive Council of Pennsylvania had neither reason nor wish to resist public clamor, and on October 27, 1780, it ordered Peggy's expulsion within 14 days as a person inimical to public safety.

The powerful Shippens tried everything that they knew to have the order rescinded. Lest her safety be risked and she be brought to trial as a traitor and, lest the whole family suffer from guilt by association, it was

A parade through the streets of Philadelphia on Saturday, September 30, 1780, in which Arnold was burned in effigy. *Courtesy of The Historical Society of Pennsylvania.*

imperative for the Shippens to underline Peggy's innocence by insisting that the order was a brutal attempt to "compel her to go to that infernal villain her husband. . . . The sacrifice was an immense one at her being married to him at all. It is much more so to be obliged, against her will, to go to the arms of a man who appears to be so very black."

Such protestations did Peggy less than justice. Her love for the United States had been short lived, and her loyalty to the American cause was easily subverted by doubts and ambitions. But there can be no question that she loved her husband and her loyalty to him was unshaken even in disaster.

Nor did the disaster seem to be entire when Peggy rejoined Arnold in New York. She may have wept a few tears for the handsome British officer who had died at Tappan; she may have sighed for the titles, the power, and the affluence that would have been hers had the conspiracy succeeded; but even for a failed traitor and his wife, life in New York was by no means harsh.

Younger and junior British officers might refuse to associate with a family that was held to be responsible for the death of André. But Clinton treated the Arnolds, who had become his next-door neighbors, with entire courtesy, and he and the government to which he was responsible fulfilled their bargain with Arnold to the last penny. Indeed, when one considers that Arnold had delivered nothing but himself and had cost the life of a brilliant and popular officer, the British behaved with remarkable generosity.

Arnold (who had collected every penny of his American pay that he could lay his hands on before he defected to the British, and who had the gall to ask for his back pay even after he had defected) received from the British £6,000 and £525 for his expenses. When the news of this payment reached Franklin in Paris he wrote to Lafayette: "Judas sold only one man, Arnold 3,000,000. Judas got for his one man 30 pieces of silver, Arnold not a halfpenny a head. A miserable bargainer." From his different point of view Arnold agreed with Franklin and, just as he had previously complained of the meanness of his American masters, so now and for the rest of his days he was loud in his criticism of the miserliness of the British, lamenting in particular that he had not been compensated for the loss of his prospects, investments, or for the confiscation of his Philadelphia property. When he was an American merchant, when he was an American officer, and when he was a British officer, Arnold always lived beyond his means and was always hagridden by his debts. Yet from the moment of his defection Arnold was paid by the British as a cavalry colonel with a supplement as a provincial brigadier. Like most other colonels he went on half pay at the end of the war but, unusually, he was also allowed half of his supplement. Peggy and her young child were given pensions for life; so too was another child, born in New York. Though none was more than 12 years old, Arnold's three sons by his first marriage were immediately commissioned in the British army. Young Benedict was promoted to lieutenant in 1783 and in 1795 died of wounds received fighting against the French. The other two boys remained in America with their aunt and never soldiered in the British army, but they continued to draw half pay until they died, Henry in New York in 1826 and Richard in Canada in 1847—almost 70 years after his father's uncompleted service at West Point.

(The conscience of the British government was remarkably acute: André's three sisters were also given pensions and his brother was knighted.)

But, even while he whined about the poor financial recompense, Arnold demonstrated also the other, the brave side of his remarkable nature. Almost as soon as he settled in New York, British intelligence reported American plans to kidnap him, and his own military sense was alert to the certainty that, if he exposed himself to the risk of capture in battle, the dangers that he must face would be far greater than those of any other officer in the British service. Wisdom and the advice of his few Loyalist friends dictated that he give up the war and move to the safety of England. Instead he stayed in New York, preparing for the British high command elaborate memoranda on the future conduct of the war. These contained a strange mixture of military wisdom and political fatuousness (one proposed bribing Washington with a peerage) and included always as an essential prerequisite high rank for Benedict Arnold.

Finally he was unleashed by Clinton and in the two last campaigns of his life, into Virginia and against his homeland Connecticut, he behaved with his customary military vigor but also with such ferocity as to feed the distaste for him that was general among his British colleagues. This almost inconceivably added a new dimension of horror to the hate which from the beginning of his career had never been far below the surface of American feelings toward him, the hate which at the time of the treason at West Point had enshrined his as the most loathed name in American history.

Even when Clinton's dilatoriness, the skill of Washington and Rochambeau, and the intervention of the Almighty who kept the relieving British fleet away from the mouth of the York River, settled the fate of Cornwallis's army, Arnold still refused to believe that the war was over. Still he had a plan to bring the Americans back to their senses and himself to proper recognition.

He was allowed to go to England to present his scheme to the government but was met with no support and little friendship.

Three times in the years when Britain faced the armies of the French Revolution, Arnold tried for a command, but no government, opposition, or army relished the prospect of placing British troops under an American traitor. He tried living among the United Empire Loyalists in the province of New Brunswick but found there the climate of opinion among erstwhile Americans as uncongenial as the weather; and although the British government relented so far as to give him a large grant of land in Upper Canada, he never visited his property.

On June 12, 1801, Benedict Arnold died in London. "Poor General Arnold has departed this world without notice" wrote one newspaper; and another described him "as a person much noticed during the American War."

On August 24, 1803, after years of illness and months of agony, Peggy Shippen Arnold died of cancer.

The issue of American loyalty was settled at Yorktown, but Arnold's chance to be numbered among the great of history had vanished in the moment when he left John André to his fate. With time the passions faded; there could be recognition, even sorrow, for Arnold's wasted courage and for the military skills so prodigally thrown away. But for all time Arnold's fame is his infamous treachery. And, though passion has vanished, still now as in 1780 the hero of the story is its tragic victim and, in American and British history alike, there lingers on a note of mourning for the death of John André.

Appendix A:
"The Ballad of Major André"

Come all you brave Americans
And unto me give ear,
I sing you now a ditty
That will your spirits cheer
Concerning a young gentleman who went to Tarry town
Where he met a British officer
A man of high renown.

Then up stepped this young hero,
John Paulding was his name,
'Oh tell us where you're going sir
And also whence you came.'
'I bear the British flag sir,'
Up-answered bold André,
'I have a pass that takes me through,
I have no time to stay.'

Then others came around him
And bade him to dismount,

'Come tell us where you're going,
Give us a strict account.'
Young Paulding said, 'We are resolved
That you shall ne'er pass by'.
And so the evidence did prove
The prisoner a spy.

He begged for his liberty
He pled for his discharge
And often times he told them
If they set him at large
He'd give the gold and silver
He had laid up in store
And when he reached the city
He would send them ten times more.

'We want no gold and silver
You have laid up in store,'
Van Wart and Paulding both did cry,
'You need not send us more'.
He saw that his conspiracy
Would soon be brought to light
He begged for pen and paper
And asked for to write.

The story came to Arnold
Commanding at the Fort,
He called for the *Vulture*
And sailed for New York.
Now Arnold to New York he came
To fight for his King,
And left poor Major André
On the gallows for to swing.

André was executed
He looked both meek and mild
His face was fair and handsome
And pleasantly he smiled
It moved each eye with pity
And every heart there bled
And everyone wished him released
And Arnold in his stead.

He was a man of honor
In Britain he was born
To die upon the gallows
Most highly he did scorn
And now his life has reached its end
So young and blooming still
In Tappan's quiet countryside
He sleeps upon the hill.

Appendix B:
Lieut. John Whiting

An American officer, Lieut. John Whiting, comments on Arnold's treachery:*

The night of the 25 inst. Col. Robertson[1] with five hundred Men was to pass by Verplank's point dressed like our Troops under a pretence of a reinforcement from our army: at Robertson's house Arnold was to be surprised. General Washington, the Marquis de la Fayette, the Chevalier de la Luzerne, ambassador, B. Genl. Knox, all their aids and attendants were to be taken, after which they were to take possession of West Point, which [torn] much resistance the Garrison being reduced (would you believe it) to about three hundred Militia, besides Artillery, having under various pretences been distributed *here* and *there*—two hundred cutting wood at one place. The soldiers in the Garrison had not more than two Cartridges per man, having been divested of them under the plausible pretence that two was enough to stand on Sentry: had they more they would waste them—no alarm post was assigned to any but the

---

[1]Col. Beverley Robinson, a Loyalist, whose mansion on the Hudson was occupied by Arnold as his headquarters. He fled with Arnold to England, and died at Thornbury in 1792.

*From *Massachusetts Historical Society Collections*, 1892.

Artillery. You see how easily this might have taken place; but can you discern how near the brink of ruin we were? Men at the head of our military affairs with illustrious Foreigners captured; the communication between the States cut off:—The treachery was to be kept a secret and Arnold after receiving his reward was to have his Parole and return to his Seat in Philadelphia to spend in his former luxurious manner the Judas-like gain. Mr. Andrie and Mr. Smith are to be tried today. Andrie was one of their most promising officers in the British Service and had attained the rank of Major from a Lieutenant by particular merits.

How propitious! how merciful! is indulgent heaven in [*torn and illegible*] the almost inconceivable depravity of human nature which cautions [*torn*] not to rest secure in human faith without suffering us to purchase our [*torn*] dearly by experience. Would time allow [*torn*] further relation of so despicable [*torn*] how the public Stores were disposed of by Genl. Arnold.

Mrs. Warren lent him twenty-two thousand dollars which he left unpaid.

Many Persons say they were not deceived in Genl. Arnold: I confess I had a good opinion of him as an Officer in the Field, but ever thought him to be ambitious and possest of a great degree of avarice and luxury. Some imagine his profuse manner of living had so involved him in debt that poverty urged him to it. Enough upon so perfidious a person. Leave him to his fate and admire the Man who bears to be honest in the worst of times.

Appendix C: Excerpt from Thacher's Military Journal during the American Revolutionary War, 1775-1783

"Arnold remains the solitary instance of an American officer who abandoned the side first embraced in the contest and turned his sword on his former companions in arms." "I am mistaken," says Washington in a letter to a friend, "if at this time Arnold is undergoing the torments of a mental hell. From some traits of his character which have lately come to my knowledge, he seems to have been so hacknied in crime; so lost to all sense of honor and shame, that while his faculties still enable him to continue his sordid pursuits, there will be no time for remorse." "This man," says Hamilton, "is in every sense despicable. In addition to the scene of knavery and prostitution during his command at

Philadelphia, which the late seizure of his papers has unfolded, the history of his command at West Point is a history of little as well as of great villanies. He practised every dirty act of peculation, and even stooped to connexions with the sutlers of the garrison to defraud the public." A respectable officer, in a letter to a friend, speaks of Arnold in the following language. "It is not possible for human nature to receive a greater quantity of guilt than he possesses. Perhaps there is not a single obligation, moral or divine, but what he has broken through. It is discovered now, that in his most early infancy, hell marked him for her own, and infused into him a full proportion of her own malice. His late apostacy is the summit of his character. He began his negotiations with the enemy, to deliver up West Point to them, long before he was invested with the command of it, and whilst he was still in Philadelphia; after which, he solicited the command of that post from the ostensible cause that the wound in his leg incapacitated him for an active command in the field." His papers contain the most authentic and incontestable proofs of his crime, and that he regarded his important employments only as affording him opportunities to pillage the public with impunity. The crimes of this unprincipled conspirator are thus summed up. Treason, avarice, hypocrisy, ingratitude, barbarity, falsehood, deception, peculation and robbery. He aimed to plunge a dagger into the bosom of his country, which had raised him from the obscurity in which he was born, to honors which never could have been the object even of his hopes. He robbed his country at the time of her deepest distress, having directed his wife to draw all she could from the commissaries' store, and sell or store it, though at a time when the army was destitute of provisions. He robbed the soldiers when they were in want of necessaries and defrauded his own best friends who trusted and had rendered him the most essential services. He spoke contemptuously of our allies, the French, and his illiberal abuse of every character opposed to his fraudulent and wicked transactions exceeds all description. For the sake of human nature it were to be wished that a veil could forever be thrown over such a vile example of depravity and wickedness. An effigy of Arnold, large as life, was constructed by an artist at Philadelphia and seated in a cart, with the figure of the devil at his elbow, holding a lantern up to the face of the traitor to show him to the people, having his name and crime in capital letters. The cart was paraded the whole evening through the streets of the city with drums and fifes playing the rogue's march, with other marks of infamy, and was attended by a vast concourse of people. The effigy was finally hanged for the want of the original, and then committed to the flames. Yet this is the man on whom the British have bestowed ten thousand pounds sterling as the price of his treason, and appointed to the rank of brigadier general in their service. It could scarcely be imagined that there was an officer of honor left in that army, who would debase himself and his commission by serving under or ranking with *Benedict Arnold!* In January, 1781, Arnold was by Sir Henry Clinton invested with the command of one thousand seven hundred men, supported by a naval force, on an expedition to Virginia, where he committed extensive ravages on the rivers and along the unprotected coast, plundering the plantations to the extent of his power. According to report he shipped off a cargo of negroes, which he had stolen, to Jamaica, and sold them for his own emolument. Having taken an American captain prisoner, he inquired of him, what the Americans would do with him if he should fall into their hands; the officer replied, they would cut off the leg that was wounded at Saratoga and bury it with the honors of war, and hang the remainder of his body on a gibbet. In September, 1781, Arnold was again vested with a command and sent on a predatory expedition against New London, in Connecticut, his native state. After taking possession of the fort, they made a merciless slaughter of the men who defended it, and destroyed an immense quantity of provisions, stores and shipping; sixty dwelling houses and eighty four stores were destroyed, and about one hundred inhabitants were deprived of their habitations and most of them of their all. This terminated the career of this monster of wickedness in America. At the close of the war, he accompanied the royal army to England. "The contempt that followed him through life," says a late elegant writer, * "is further illustrated by the speech of the present Lord Lauderdale, who, perceiving Arnold on the right hand of the king, and near his person, as he addressed his parliament, declared, on his return to the commons, that however gracious the language he had heard from the throne, his indignation could not but be highly excited, at beholding as he had done, his majesty supported by a traitor." "And on another occasion, Lord Surry, since duke of Norfolk, rising to speak in the house of commons, and perceiving Arnold in the gallery, sat down with precipitation, exclaiming, 'I will not speak while that man, pointing to him, is in the house '"

He purchased in England a quantity of goods which he brought over to New Brunswick, the store and goods took fire, and the whole were consumed; but according to report they were insured to a much greater amount than their real value. After this event no further laurels remained for him to achieve; he recrossed the Atlantic and died in London, June 14th, 1801.

From: James Thatcher, Military Journal during the American Revolutionary War, 1775-1783: Richardard & Lord (Boston, 1823).

Additional Reading

Alden, J. R. *The American Revolution, 1775–1783.* New York: Harper, 1954.

Arnold, I. N. *The Life of Benedict Arnold.* Chicago: McClurg, 1879.

Billias, George A. (ed.). *George Washington's Generals.* New York: Morrow, 1964.

Clinton, Sir Henry. *The American Rebellion* (ed. William B. Willcox). New Haven: Yale Univ. Press, 1954.

Flexner, James T. *The Traitor and the Spy.* New York: Harcourt, 1953.

Freeman, Douglas Southall. *George Washington* (6 vols.). New York: Scribner's, 1948–1952.

Hacker, Louis. *Alexander Hamilton in the American Tradition.* New York: McGraw-Hill, 1957.

Miller, John C. *Triumph of Freedom 1775–1783.* Boston: Little Brown (Atlantic Monthly Press), 1948.

Nye, R. B., and Morpurgo, J. E. *The Birth of the U.S.A.* London and Baltimore: Penguin, 1955, 3rd rev. edn., 1970.

Peckham, Howard. *The War for Independence: A Military History.* Chicago: Univ. of Chicago Press, 1958.

Robson, Eric. *The American Revolution in Its Political and Military Aspects, 1763–1783.* New York: Oxford Univ. Press, 1955.

Sargent, Winthrop. *The Life and Career of Major John André.* New York: Somerset Publishers, 1972 (rpt of 1902 ed.).

Smith, Joshua Hett. *Narrative of the Causes Which Led to*

the Death of Major John André. New York: Arno Press, 1969 (rpt. of 1808 ed.).

Smith, Paul H. *Loyalists and Redcoats: A Study in British Revolutionary Policy.* Chapel Hill, N.C.: Univ. of North Carolina Press, 1964.

Tillotson, Harry S. *The Beloved Spy: The Life and Loves of Major John André.* Caldwell, Ida.: Caxton, 1948.

Van Doren, Carl. *Secret History of the American Revolution.* New York: Viking, 1941.

Wallace, Willard M. *Traitorous Hero: The Life and Fortunes of Benedict Arnold.* New York: Harper, 1948.

———. *Appeal to Arms: A Military History of the American Revolution.* New York: Harper, 1951.

Wright, Esmond. *Washington and the American Revolution.* New York: Macmillan, 1957.

Index